INLINE SKATING

INLINE SKATING

JEREMY EVANS

With photos by Matt Pingel

PARRAGON

This is a Parragon Book

© Parragon 1998

Parragon
13 Whiteladies Road
Clifton, Bristol BS8 1PB
United Kingdom

Designed, produced and packaged by
Touchstone
Old Chapel Studio, Plain Road, Marden, Tonbridge,
Kent TN12 9LS United Kingdom

Edited by Philip de Ste. Croix

ISBN 0-75252-547-6

Printed in Italy

Contents

Introduction

Inline skating has taken the concept of self-propelled wheels into a new dimension, providing an effortless, positive response which allows skaters of the most basic ability to move with grace, speed and style – and feel good about doing it. A huge attraction is that you can do it any place where there is a smooth, hard surface, and if you're that smitten, you can even do it offroad!

The reality, unfortunately, can be a little different. While those living in urban areas – which means most of us – generally have plenty of smooth tarmac, the very popularity of the sport has created something of a fatal attraction. The 'Ban All Skaters' brigade has never been far behind, and in some areas it has been successful in implementing notorious and draconian bans, such as the closure of most of London's Royal Parks to skaters.

▷ *The peak years for aggressive skaters are those when fear doesn't exist!*

No matter. People will keep on skating, the sport will continue to grow at a huge rate, wider acceptance will come, better facilities will be created, and in time all skaters will be allowed to go about their business and co-exist in hassle-free harmony with other users of tarmac. It's all about the right to enjoy life's little – and not so little – pleasures, but at the same time taking care not to adopt a selfish attitude to others which would curtail their own enjoyment or freedom of movement.

This is not a new problem for fresh, dynamic young sports, and it can be beaten. The difficulty lies is persuading and converting established local authorities, which are so often dominated by older people who have no concept of the joy of inline skating, don't want anything to do with it, and simply dismiss the sport as a branch of current youth culture which they can do without.

We know they are wrong. Inline skating is not just about kids whose wishes can be ignored. It is a sport which offers everyone a brilliant way to get up off the couch, whizz around outside, have fun, get fit, get involved, develop skills and learn team-work. Kids as young as five or six years old can learn to skate well, and with all the right padding and protection adults can start to skate safely when they are collecting their pensions. And in between those ages, skating is no less important as a way that those around their teen years can avoid the trap of urban boredom which creates so many problems in contemporary society.

Don't get the impression that inline skating is confined to certain age groups. For sure, the peak

years for aggressive skaters, who like to 'grind' rails and get 'air' off ramps, are teens the and early 20s when fear doesn't exist and the body can be pushed to its wildest limits. Hockey players and speed skaters can start just as young but stay competitive much longer, building up a lifetime of skills based on experience which will see them playing and racing well into their 40s and 50s. Recreational skating – mainly known as 'Rec' – is just about the fun of cruising on wheels, and becomes 'fitness' skating for those who like to take their exercise more seriously.

All of this is inline skating, and it is open to all ages. To qualify, you just have to get through the basics of pushing off, turning and stopping – all easy techniques which most people can learn to handle in half a dozen sessions. Once up and running, you will then want nothing more than to enjoy the feel of your wheels and to get better. And to learn to skate faster, turn tighter, stop faster, skate through slalom cones (just use tin cans) forwards and maybe backwards, learn about going up and down hills, and perhaps move on to a few tricks like 180s or 360s.

By that stage, you're well able to decide when and where you want to go, and – if that's your wish – to branch off into the aggressive, hockey or speed disciplines.

CAUTION!

◆ *Always wear protective equipment.*

◆ *Skate within your capabilities.*

◆ *Only skate where it is safe.*

◆ *Beware of all traffic.*

◆ *Be courteous and sensitive to non-skaters.*

◆ *Skate to give skating a good name!*

How Inline Skating Developed

Like many good (and some not so good) things, inline skating started in the USA and then spread Worldwide. The whole concept was developed by two crafty, ingenious and innovative brothers called Scott and Brennan Olson from Minneapolis. They were looking for some means for ice hockey players to keep up their dedicated training in the off-season when all the natural ice had disappeared during the warmer months of the year, and hit on the idea of replacing each ice skate's blades with a line of wheels that would give a similar feel.

In fact they were not the first people to give it a go – no way! Ice skating was extremely popular in France and Holland in the 18th century, and there are old illustrations of two-wheeled off-ice contraptions which were of course very primitive, and, one suspects, very uncomfortable. A man called Robert Tyers developed the idea with a full five-wheel version which appeared in England in 1823, but it wasn't until the late 19th century invention of bearings to help wheels run smoothly that roller skates began to develop in their own right. These four-wheeled skates were arranged in a 2+2 pattern which is why they are now widely known as 'quads', and they became a long-running rage throughout Europe and the USA.

However, quads never had the smooth, flowing feel of ice skates which allow you to glide in such a perfect, synchronized motion, while hitting high speed and cutting spectacular manoeuvres. The Olsons and their inline wheel concept overcame this, effectively cloning the ice-skating sensation while managing to include three big improvements in their innovative package. First, inliners are potentially faster than ice skates because their highly developed wheels spin much more easily than a blade cuts through ice. Second, due to this low, rolling resistance, inlines are easier to power up, making inlining an easier sport to learn with fluid forward motion soon achieved after the first few shaky steps. Third, you don't need ice to skate. Any good, smooth surface will do, and as we all know – there's a lot of tarmac out there today!

The Olson brothers had enough faith and foresight to make their invention a production reality, and, what is more, they hit on a brilliant name for the new sports concept, calling their product a 'Rollerblade'. The name is still in use today and Rollerblade remains one of the world's biggest inline manufacturers, although now owned by the Italian company Benetton.

Rollerblade began volume manufacture in 1980 with a model which apart from its front stopper wouldn't look too out of place today. Having successfully targeted the ice hockey market, it did not take the Olson brothers long to realize that a far wider application was possible than the comparatively specialist role of off-ice training.

This was a new kind of sport, a new kind of fun in itself, and what's more it was accessible to a huge urban and suburban population which had sufficient money to enjoy this new recreation. Of course Rollerblade couldn't hold the market alone. Other businessmen and innovators stormed onto the bandwagon with their own versions of the same concept, while the name of the sport evolved into 'inlining'. From there on, it has conquered the world – or at least the relatively rich parts of the world which have plenty of smooth tarmac to skate on – with a guesstimated 30 million or more people out there skating on inlines today.

△ *Hockey was where it started, when the Olson brothers invented a way for players to train without ice. It is now a huge game in its own right.*

▷ *The urban and suburban population took to inline skates, and developed their own forms of the sport such as aggressive skating.*
◁

THERE'S A LOT OF TARMAC OUT THERE!

Inline Skating Today

Roller-skating on quads came and went as a popular passion, as did skateboarding, although a dedicated minority still pursue both these interests which have something of a cult status. Inline skating is different. It has become huge by comparison, with almost 4 million pairs of skates being sold during 1997 in Europe alone. Furthermore, these were 'quality' skates which hit a certain price point and excluded the so-called 'toy skates', the cheap imitations sold in toy shops for children which offer poor quality in every respect.

▷ *The accomplished street skater uses every facility to pursue this sport in the urban environment.*

The big names in worldwide skate production include names such as Rollerblade and Roces (Italy), Roller Derby and Ultra Wheels (USA), Bauer (Canada), K2 (Germany) and Inliners (UK). In addition there are dozens of specialist companies, such as Razors and Oxygen (aggressive skates), CCM, Mission and Franklin (hockey skates, clothing and equipment), and Hyper and Kryptonics (every type of wheel you can imagine). They add up to a huge market, which in recent times has experienced a profound shift in emphasis with 'aggressive' skates moving ahead as the biggest-selling sector of the market, in place of the recreational, fitness and junior (children's) skates which started it all rolling.

This trend has posed its own problems. The recreational/fitness/junior market should provide a firm foundation for the sport to grow on, before second-generation skaters acquire the knowledge to branch into different specialist directions. Instead, that firm foundation has been hijacked by the aggressive market, while the hockey and speed sectors remain relatively small. The result is that inline skating is now perceived by many outsiders as a hardcore sport for tough urban kids with an absolute maximum age of 20, rather than a sport which all ages and abilities can enjoy without

◁ △ *Ramp tricks allow skaters to literally fly through the air.*

necessarily being expected to slide down hand-rails or wage war with security guards in car parks.

The skate manufacturers are worried by this trend, being fearful of burn-out when the kids get bored of the aggressive style of inlining and opt to move on to some new thrill. It's just what happened to skateboarding all those years ago, but the difference is that inline skating has a much more user-friendly base which appeals to all ages. It also has far wider applications which range from skating to work, skating to play, skating to play hockey, skating to race round a track, and even skating to ride a street course or fly off a half pipe. While inline skating may be due for a melt-down, it certainly won't go away!

△ *Drop-ins, flips and grinds are all part of the extensive aggressive repertoire.*

Inline Skates

SKATE ELEMENTS
All inline skates combine a similar mix of elements:

Outer Boot
Most skates have a hard moulded polyurethane plastic outer boot (also known as a 'shell'), with a high, hinged cuff at the top to allow for movement and to provide support for the ankle with an adjustable 'power strap' fed through a buckle at the side of the shin. The exceptions are stitched leather boots which are mainly used for hockey, and 'soft boots' which aim to combine the looks and comfort of trainers with an internal rigid skeleton providing the necessary support.

Buckles & Laces
Adjustable buckle systems are widely used for inline skates. They offer a precise and easy fastening which locks shut and often uses a ratchet mechanism to make the buckle tighter. All the major manufacturers have their own buckle designs which work pretty well, but some aggressive skaters and many hockey skaters still prefer the old 'ice-style' laces which offer more precise control. Laces are considerably more of a fiddle when it comes to putting on or taking off a boot, but they are totally reliable in an impact, unlike buckles which may come undone or get broken. Aluminium buckles are considerably stronger than plastic in this respect.

Soft inner boot

Inner boot
All skates with an outer boot also have an inner boot which is a cross between a thick foam sock with a tongue and a soft boot that you could wear indoors. Inner boots are removable for washing, and cushion your feet to make the skates as comfortable and close-fitting as possible. An inner boot should ideally be made of a specialist material such as Coolmax which helps conduct perspiration away from the feet via ventilation holes cut in the outer boot, and which has a 'memory' which returns the boot to its original shape after use.

Adjustable buckles

Hinged cuff

Hard outer boot

Heel brake

Chassis/frame

Wheels and bearings

Insole
The insole or footbed is a replaceable cushioned pad which lines the bottom of the outer boot. A high quality orthopedic footbed offers the best levels of arch support, cushions the foot against shock, helps conduct perspiration away and maintains its performance for extended use.

Chassis

The chassis (also known as a 'frame') carries the wheels on steel axles and brass or nylon spacers, and acts as the 'blade' on which you skate. It must be very strong, very light and as torsionally rigid and stiff as possible. Favoured materials are glass-filled nylon such as Zytel, although aluminium and occasionally carbon may be used for super light requirements. Different chassis take different wheel sizes. Some have a 'rockering' feature with aluminium rocker washers which are turned to let the middle wheels drop lower or higher in the chassis.

Brake

The first Rollerblades were fitted with a toe brake in the style also favoured by quads. This was soon superseded by the heel brake which, at its simplest, is a rubber block mounted on the back of the chassis. The technique is to lift the front of the skate so the rubber brake touches the ground, applying more or less force to vary the braking effort. The rubber brake pad should be regularly checked for wear, and replaced as necessary.

It is usual to have just one brake fitted to whichever skate suits as the 'braking foot'. Refinements include brakes which can be 'dialled down' to renew the braking surface as it wears, and brakes which are activated as the shin pulls back on the top cuff. Other systems, such as a hand-held, electronic brake, have been tried with rather less success.

There is a growing movement among experienced skaters to do away with a brake altogether. They believe that a brake interferes with techniques such as cross-overs, that other stopping techniques are superior and – more to the point – it doesn't look cool. All this is to some extent true, but it goes without saying that the ability to stop is of vital importance in terms of safety. If in doubt you should have a brake system available.

RECREATIONAL SKATES

Entry-level skates for all-round use make the least demands on a skater and skate manufacturer, and are available at the lowest price points.

A good recreational skate should include the following features:
◆ *Hard-wearing outer boot to withstand scrapes and scratches while learning on tarmac.*
◆ *High-cut, hinged cuff with power strap for full flexible ankle support.*
◆ *Easy adjustment and closure by buckles.*
◆ *Soft, removable inner boot and insole.*
◆ *Glass-filled nylon chassis with heel brake as standard.*
◆ *Wheels around 76mm 82A fitted with ABEC 1 bearings for reliable performance (see pages 16-19 for an explanation of this terminology).*

KIDS' STARTER SKATES

Kids from five years and upwards are best served by scaled-down recreational skates, though they may prefer something closer in style to the aggressive skates of their peers. As with all kids' footwear, rapidly growing feet present a problem when it comes to the cost of a pair of skates. Some manufacturers have attempted to overcome this by producing adjustable boots which cover up to four full junior sizes, and they work surprisingly well.

Look for these features in kid's skates:
◆ *Hard-wearing outer boot to withstand scrapes, scratches and plenty of misuse on tarmac.*
◆ *High, hinged cuff with power strap for full ankle support.*
◆ *Easy closure and adjustment by means of buckles.*
◆ *Soft, removable inner boot and inside.*
◆ *Glass-filled nylon chassis with heel brake as standard, though it has to be said that when skating in a safe environment many kids manage well enough with no brake at all.*
◆ *Wheels around 70mm 82A fitted with ABEC 1 bearings*

FITNESS SKATES

This type of skate is moving up a league from recreational skates, catering to second- and third-generation skaters who know what they want and are willing to invest in the best possible performance. Fitness skates are likely to be much the same in style as recreational skates, but designed and fitted to more exacting levels.

Make sure the skates fit and are as comfortable as possible with good support at the ankles.

Important features that fitness skates should include:

◆ *The choice of hard-boot or soft-boot technology. Rigid ankle support becomes less important for more experienced skaters who may prefer the lighter weight and more relaxed feel and appearance of a soft boot. They should be experienced enough to guarantee it will not get dragged across tarmac.*

◆ *Lightweight, rigid, glass-filled nylon or aluminium chassis, rockerable axles, and heel brake removed for manoeuvres.*

◆ *Wheels around 76mm 78A with better grip and power, fitted with bearings up to ABEC 5 for top performance. High-level fitness skaters may opt to go all the way with a stretched five-wheel aluminium chassis taking oversize 80mm 78A wheels for maximum speed at the expense of poor manoeuvrability.*

SPEED SKATES

Top class racing is a very specific discipline which demands a unique style of skate.

A typical speed skate specification would be:

◆ *Hand-stitched, lace-up leather boot cut low on the ankle with rigid carbon base.*

◆ *Long 325mm (12.80in) super light and totally rigid aluminium chassis fitted with five 80mm wheels with zero axle clearance between the wheels and sole, and choice of wheel hardness depending on race surfaces from 78A to 86A with ABEC 5 bearings.*

▷ *Look for the 5-wheel set-up of dedicated speed skates.*

When the skate fits

◆ *It is vital, above all else, to get skates that fit and are comfortable. You may set your heart on a certain model, but all feet are different and if the skate doesn't feel right, it's not right for you. Always try on the skates, do them up, and if possible have a little roll round the shop.*

◆ *A skate should grip tightly at the ankle where it gives maximum support. The boot should be a close fit so your foot is held firmly while you are wearing thin socks, with your toes just kissing the ends. Don't do buckles or laces up so tightly that you cut off the blood supply and make your foot go numb.*

◆ *Skate sizes tend to be expressed in UK, American and European measurements. American sizes are about one size smaller than UK sizes – for instance an American 11 equates to a UK 10.*

HOCKEY SKATES

Hockey players have tended to prefer a traditional ice hockey-style boot that features stitched leather (or synthetic leather) and ballistic nylon construction with a plastic toe cap, lace fastenings and maximum ventilation. This provides the lightest possible skate which moulds to the foot for precise energy transmission without foot slippage or excess weight. The downside is that while an ice hockey boot will slide on ice without damage, the same style will be prone to shred on tarmac and will also abrade when sliding on a wooden sports-court floor.

Some manufacturers produce hybrid composite boots in the lower price ranges which feature plastic (polyurethane) moulded bottoms combined with stitched tops – they even have imitation stitches in the plastic! Other manufacturers are promoting full hard-boot technology for hockey, combining lace fastenings with a power strap around the hinged cuff. Both types are likely to be harder wearing, but heavier and less sensitive, than the classic stitched boot hockey style.

△ Hockey skates owe a lot to ice hockey designs.

AGGRESSIVE SKATES

Aggressive skates provide the biggest challenge to a manufacturer since they get the hardest life. Most of the problems are caused by 'grinding' – sliding on hand rails or kerbs – which puts a huge amount of strain on the chassis and any part of the boot that makes contact.

▷ *The aggressive skate is chunky and tough.*

Typical elements of a top-class aggressive skate will include:

◆ *Hard-boot construction with a hinged cuff cut low for more effective manoeuvres, but still holding the ankle firmly. Removable cuff and main shell for easy replacement when damaged.*

◆ *Plenty of soul space (flat sole of the boot to slide on) and heel block area (flat heel to slide on) to 'lock on' when grinding.*

◆ *Lace fastening for the main boot to provide a secure, no-slip fit at all times, with a power strap and secure locking clip providing precise adjustment round the shin area.*

◆ *Low profile, glass-reinforced nylon chassis, fully rockerable, and allowing an adjustable grind area gap between the middle two wheels. It should be attached to the boot with counter-sunk rivets which will not wear away on grinds.*

◆ *Small 57mm wheels for maximum manoeuvrability and control. Possibility of combining soft 88A wheels on the outside and hard 92A wheels on the inside.*

◆ *Replaceable plastic grind plates and an H-block to protect the central area of chassis while grinding, or a reinforced pre-grooved frame.*

General features for a good hockey boot will include:

◆ *Classic stitched construction or hard-boot technology with a hinged cuff. On a stitched boot, the cuff is cut low for easy movement with a tab for support at the back, acknowledging that good hockey players have pretty strong ankles anyway.*

◆ *Lace-up fastening for a precise fit which will not come undone, used with a power strap on a hard boot with a hinged cuff.*

◆ *Lightweight, super-rigid magnesium, aluminium or glass-reinforced nylon chassis with rockerable axles. No heel brake.*

◆ *Wheels around 76mm 84A, depending on type of surface to be played, with bearings up to ABEC 5 for top performance.*

▷ *Aggressive skates are subject to daily doses of misuse and maltreatment. They need to be tough to survive!*

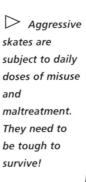

Skate Equipment

WHEELS

Wheel sizes

The size of a skate wheel is measured in millimetres (mm) on the outside diameter of the wheel. Smaller wheels will tend to turn and accelerate more quickly, with excellent response to sudden changes in direction and heavy loading. They do not have high top-end speed. Larger wheels will tend to be slower to accelerate and less manoeuvrable, but have a much higher top-end speed. Wheel sizes range from the smallest (around 47mm) for aggressive skating, through wheels for children (around 60mm), up to general recreational and fitness skating wheels (around 72mm), with top-end speed skaters using the biggest wheels for racing (around 80m).

Wheel hardness

The 'durometer' (hardness) of a wheel can range from 74A (soft) through to 100+A (hard). Durometer has a direct relation to a wheel's performance, durability, shock absorption and traction. The softer the wheel, the better the traction and the smoother the ride, but the quicker the wheel will wear down or 'chunk' (bits of the compound coming off). The harder the wheel, the faster it will go (on a good surface), but the less it will grip, with hardness also implying good wear at the expense of poor shock absorption.

	Average Wear	High Traction	Smooth Ride
74A	↕	↕	↕
78A			
82A			
88A			
100+A			
	Long Wear	Low Traction	Rough Ride

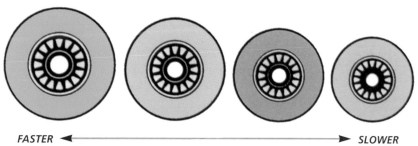

FASTER ◄──────────────► *SLOWER*

Wheel profiles

The surface of the wheel that makes contact with the ground can vary from a narrow, pointed radius for racing to a wide and virtually flat radius for aggressive skating. A narrow profile has least drag to give maximum top-end speed, but has poor stability and will wear more quickly. A wide profile is more stable but much slower, and is the preferred choice for aggressive skaters.

Wheel core

The central core of the wheel holds the bearings (contained in a cassette) in place. It is made from a very hard plastic or urethane compound which is bonded directly to the tyre. A well-designed, high quality core should promote wheel stability by preventing lateral flex, extend bearing life by protecting the cassette, and maintain the wheel's lightweight characteristics.

RACE   **HOCKEY**   **RECREATION**   **AGGRESSIVE**

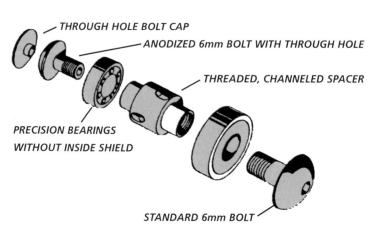

THROUGH HOLE BOLT CAP
ANODIZED 6mm BOLT WITH THROUGH HOLE
THREADED, CHANNELED SPACER
PRECISION BEARINGS WITHOUT INSIDE SHIELD
STANDARD 6mm BOLT

Wheel compounds

The outer part of the wheel – the 'tyre' – is made from a urethane compound which can be modified to produce different characteristics for different styles of skating. The chemists employed by the big wheel manufacturers have to balance the conflicting requirements of grip, speed and wear. An additional consideration is the tyre's 'rebound', which equates to how lively the skates feel under your feet on account of the shape of the wheels rebounding after every impact to return more energy to the stride that propels the skater.

Wheel durability

A good set of wheels is expensive, so long-term durability is an important consideration. In addition to the wheel's compound and profile, durability will be affected by:

◆ The skating surface – a rough surface wears wheels out more quickly than a smooth one.

◆ The weight of the skater, and how his skating style transfers that weight to the sides of the wheels.

◆ The type of skating – aggressive skating is notoriously hard on wheels, particularly in a true street environment.

Wheel rotation

The skating movement pushes from the inside of each 'blade' and consequently the inside profiles of the wheels will wear down while the outsides are less affected. There will also be different amounts of wear visible on the front, back and middle wheels.

To spread the wear and get maximum life from a set of wheels, you should rotate their positions in the chassis as soon as wear becomes obvious. Exchange Wheel 1 with Wheel 3 and Wheel 2 with Wheel 4 as shown, ▷ and also turn them so that the worn side is on the outside.

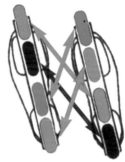

△ *Aggressive skating is the surest way to wear through a set of wheels quickly.*

Wheel rockering

'Rockering' is a surfing term which defines how much a surfboard is bent to increase its turning capacity on a wave. The concept has been borrowed by inline skating, with some chassis featuring rocker spacers which allow wheels to be dropped or lifted.

In its most usual application, a chassis can be rockered with the middle two wheels dropped so that the front and back wheels are lifted clear of the ground when the skate is horizontal, which will make the skate turn faster. Alternatively the chassis could be fitted with differently sized wheels.

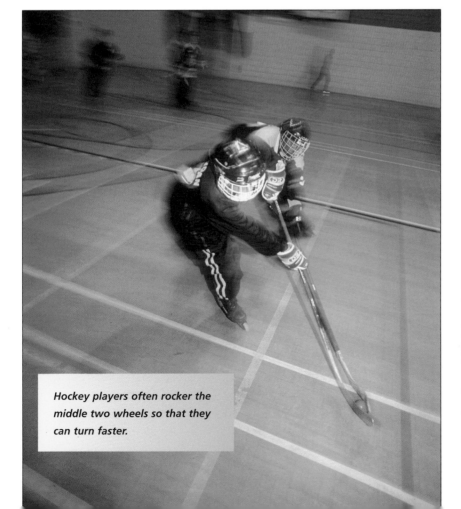

Hockey players often rocker the middle two wheels so that they can turn faster.

New for old?

It is possible to re-profile worn wheels, but they will obviously reduce in size. An amateur who attempts this operation will find it difficult to achieve a smooth profile and a consistent diameter, without access to a purpose-built tool such as the Wheel Hog re-profiling system, which is designed for use with an electric drill and is manufactured in California.

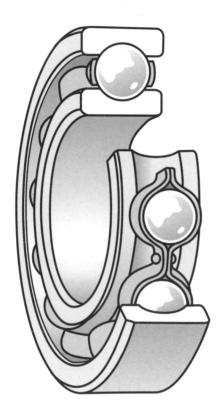

Illustration by Neil Dixon, Cthree Creative

General guidelines are as follows:
◆ ABEC 1 & 3: Up to 10,000rpm (electric drills, etc.).
◆ ABEC 5: Up to 30,000rpm (Formula 1 racing cars, etc.).
◆ ABEC 7: Up to 50,000rpm (high speed drilling).
◆ ABEC 9: Up to 120,000rpm (aerospace industry).

The higher the ABEC rating, the smoother and faster the bearing will run. What does this mean for you? It means that if you're out on your skates and hit 25mph (40kph), your 66mm wheels are running at 3,110rpm, while if you use larger 76mm wheels they run at 2,720rpm.

At the downhill loony end of the scale, if you skated at 80mph (130kph) for a long distance with good quality ABEC 5 bearings, excess heat would build up in the hub and melt the wheel unless it had a ventilated hub.

△ *Speed skaters demand the very best bearings that money can buy. They simply want to go fast.*

BEARINGS

The finer the tolerances in the bearings cassette, the better it will run, with key tolerances between the ball and the race which it spins against. The closer the ball and race, the smoother, faster and more quietly the bearings will run.

What is ABEC?

Most bearings used for inline skates claim to have an ABEC rating. ABEC is the abbreviation for the Annular Bearing Engineering Committee system which gives the bearing a precision rating on its spin. It is set up by top quality bearing manufacturers, and co-ordinated with world standards' organizations from its headquarters in Washington DC, and as such is dedicated to maintaining uniformity for all types of bearings.

The ABEC standard is intended as a guide to aid the manufacturer, customer and general public. It specifies the boundary dimensions and tolerances for running accuracy (run-out of ring track to bore or outside diameter) and internal clearance for ball bearings. These tolerances begin at ABEC 1 and end at ABEC 9. The standards are minimal requirements to ensure basic uniformity of tolerances, and most reputable manufacturers actually produce bearings which have tighter tolerances. The basic difference between ABEC 1 and 3, and 5, 7 and 9 are that the highest grades have tighter tolerances – meaning bore-to-face squareness, face-to-face parallelism and track-to-face accuracy.

△ *Reliability, rather than speed, is the main concern of aggressive skaters when it comes to getting the right bearings for the job.*

Things to consider

The ABEC label does not guarantee a set of top-quality bearings. For instance, it is possible that ABEC 1 bearings from a reliable manufacturer could be produced to a higher standard and give longer life than ABEC 5 bearings from an unknown manufacturer.

To complicate matters, an ABEC number on a bearing shield is not a guarantee of an ABEC standard, since bearings are tested for ABEC classification fully fitted with the shields in place, and rejects are possible. This means that most manufacturers do not fit shields with ABEC numbers on.

Bearing care

If bearings get wet, they will rust and their performance will deteriorate as smooth running is lost. Avoid skating in the rain, and never skate through puddles. If your wheels do get wet, try to dry out the central core area as soon as possible with a hot-air hair dryer. With extended use, bearings will start to wear down and stop spinning freely. The bearing cassette for each wheel can be removed and replaced with the aid of Allen keys and a 'bearing pusher' tool. Alternatively, a fully serviceable bearing cassette can be stripped and cleaned, but if in doubt, don't strip down or wash out a good quality set of bearings. They are assembled by the manufacturer under strict clean-room conditions, and attempting to clean them yourself may cause damage to the race-ways, by removing the protective shields or using contaminated oils. See pages 88-89 for more information on bearing replacement and maintenance.

△ *Enthusiastic skaters have to get used to stripping down their wheels, bearings and other elements.*

◁ *The bearing cassette pushes into each side of each wheel.*

▷ *Bearings on aggressive skates need to be regularly checked for smooth running.*

A number of very important items are not covered by ABEC. These include:

1. The internal design, quality and finish of a ball bearing.
2. Race curvature machining and finish.
3. Number and size of ball and surface finish.
4. Cage material and design and tolerance.
5. Material specification – grain size, cleanliness, hardness and smooth machining of all moving parts.
6. Radial play and lubrication.

Note that for the extra hard use of aggressive street and vert skating, it is essential that bearings should come from a top manufacturer which uses chrome hardened alloy steel balls and race-ways. Otherwise, inferior bearings will tend to flatten out as a result of jumping.

△ *There is a huge choice of wheels on sale. These are small aggressive wheels.*

Inline Protection

Inline skating is a safe sport, so long as you take precautions. It is possible for inexperienced skaters to travel quite fast enough for trouble to occur, and, if you fall the ground is very hard. With that in mind, it makes sense always to wear protection. You may see more than a few skaters out there who don't wear pads or wrist guards. Rest assured that only a minority of them are so skilled that they can skate safely without protection – the rest are taking the kind of risks that can cause them to end up in hospital.

▷ *Skate sensibly and safely – always wear the right level of protection.*

Degrees of risk

◆ Recreational and fitness skaters should wear knee pads and wrist guards as a matter of course. Elbow pads should also be worn, but more experienced skaters can skate safely without them.

◆ Speed skaters who race at the top end of the sport must wear helmets, but are allowed to compete without pads or wrist guards so that their body movements are unobstructed. These are highly experienced skaters who understand the consequences if they crash. Any skater taking part in an organized fun race should wear full pads, wrist guards and a helmet.

◆ Aggressive skaters must wear helmets in skate parks and competitions. They should always wear pads and wrist guards, plus extra protection such as shin guards and crash shorts with padded hips to suit their style of skating. Helmets are recommended at all times. See the Aggressive Equipment section on pages 40-41.

◆ Hockey players who play in a league have no option when it comes to wearing protection, as they cannot take part without observing the minimum requirements for safety in this fast-moving game. There is specific information on hockey protection in the Hockey Equipment section on pages 72-77.

Wrist guards and gloves

Wrist guards or protective gloves are vital accessories for two reasons:

1. If you fall forwards, you need to be able to drop onto your knees (with knee pads) and the palms of your hands without sustaining injury.

2. If you fall backwards, sprained or broken wrists are a common skate injury. When falling this way, the automatic reaction is to drop onto your outstretched fingers and palms which are held out behind you. The body is not designed to do this; your wrists are not strong enough to withstand the impact, and the result is they will make a nice 'Snap!' without sufficient support and protection.

The classic design of wrist guard is wrapped around the palm and wrist, held tightly and securely by Velcro straps with the fingers and thumb left free. The wrist is supported by rigid splints with a humped, hard plastic 'palm protector' which will allow you to skid safely on your palms with your fingers raised clear of the tarmac. Alternatively, you can buy skate mitts or gloves. Beware that while many of these look extra-stylish in thin leather or suede with design details such as kevlar patches, they often do not provide the wrist support or palm protection that the more ungainly looking wrist guards do. As such, they are really only suitable for very experienced skaters.

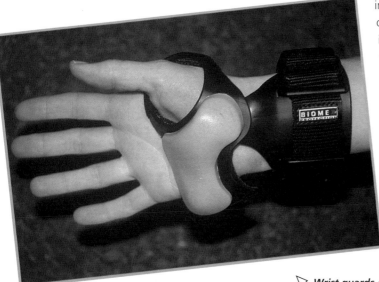

▷ *Wrist guards come in all styles, but must always combine palm and wrist protection.*

▷ *Knee pads are the first line of defence. Make sure they are secure and comfortable.*

SAFETY FIRST
◆ *Always wear suitable protection for your level of skating.*
◆ *Remember that wrist guards, pads, helmets and other protectors are only designed to reduce the risk of injury. There is no guarantee they will prevent it.*
◆ *Always 'Skate Safe' by skating within your ability.*

△ *Every impact area is protected – head, elbows, knees, wrists, palms and ankles.*

Knee and elbow pads

Knee pads are absolutely vital. The automatic safety procedure for any skater in an emergency is to drop on his knees and use them to skid to a halt, with the pads taking all the impact. Elbow pads, which are like smaller versions of knee pads, should always be worn by beginners and all those into extreme forms of skating.

A good pair of pads should be held firmly in place by adjustable webbing and Velcro straps. There should be a layer of thick padding covering the knee or elbow area, with a hard moulded plastic cap on top which will withstand everything that tarmac can do to it. The pads must not slide off the knees or elbows in the event of a fall, and the outer caps must stay secure. Most caps are held firmly in place by rivets, with some manufacturers offering stick-on caps to replace the old ones when they get worn.

Recreational skaters can generally skate safely with a set of lightweight pads. Aggressive skaters need much heavier-duty pads which protect a larger area, particularly when ramp skating where falls are heavy and frequent. In all applications it is vital that the pads are comfortable, don't chafe your skin, don't slip down your legs or arms, don't restrict the skating movement, and offer maximum padding and protection without being uncomfortably hot and sweaty.

Recreational & Fitness Skating

Recreational skating is where it starts. Put on your skates, go for a spin, enjoy the feeling, develop technique, meet friends and have a great time. Whether it's Hyde Park, Venice Beach or downtown Munich, recreational skaters the world over are cruising paths, promenades and traffic-free streets, as they enjoy a sport without barriers that's available to all ages.

Fitness skating takes the sport to a higher level. This is about more than a gentle skate, and even more than an everyday workout on wheels. Fitness skaters are a growing breed of experienced recreational skaters who understand and appreciate the value of top-quality design, materials and components. They want to skate with the best equipment available, pushing fit and function to new limits as they explore the possibilities of a more serious purpose to skating…

Skate Session

BEFORE YOU GO

Where are you going to skate? The best place is a park, well away from traffic, where there's room for you to learn and space enough to co-exist with other park-users, such as pedestrians. An ideal solution for beginners is to skate along a flat, smooth stretch of tarmac next to grass, so you can 'run-out' and stop by stepping off onto the grass.

FALLING

At the beginning you will fall; if you don't, you are not really trying. Learn to fall properly, using your knee pads and wrist guards to make it comfortable.

◆ Avoid falling backwards. It is uncomfortable, with plenty of potential for a bruised backside and the possibility of hurting your wrists. It's simple to avoid this – just keep your body bent forward in the correct 'skating stance' which is the first technique you need to learn.

◆ If you start to fall, bend your knees to drop onto your knee pads and let them absorb the initial impact. Stretch your arms forward and let the elbow pads take the secondary impact. Follow them with the wrist guards, using the reinforced humps on the palms to absorb the impact as you skid on the ground. Always keep your fingers and chin lifted to ensure they do not hit the ground.

◆ You will obviously need to get up again. It's undignified, but the easiest way to start is on all fours with your knee pads and wrist guards on the ground. Lift one knee and get the skate under you, pushing your body upright until you are kneeling on one knee with your hands by your sides. Then push up and stand up, taking care to keep your weight forwards.

SKATING STANCE

Lower your centre of gravity by bending your knees and ankles forwards. You also must bend forwards at the waist. This stance will optimize your balance, with your centre of gravity positioned over your skates. It should be maintained at all times when learning.

SKATE CHECK

◆ *Make sure there is nothing loose on your skates, and the axles and bolts are fully tight.*

◆ *Check the bearings spin freely. If they run slow or grind, you will need to give them a clean (see pages 92-93) or replace them.*

◆ *Check for wheel wear. Change the wheels round to even out the rate of wear (see pages 16-17), or replace them.*

◆ *Make sure the brake block is properly fitted with the brake bolt tight.*

◆ *Check the brake block for wear. Move it down for better contact if it is adjustable, or replace it.*

PUSH OFF AND GO

Feeling OK? All clear ahead? You are now ready to take your first skating stride. Push outwards and slightly back with your right skate, and let yourself glide with your full weight on your left skate. To complete the movement, circle your right skate back under your body. Then repeat the movement with your left skate, pushing off, putting your weight on your right skate, and bringing the left skate back under your body.

Build up a rhythm. Push off on the left, weight on the right, bring back the left, push off on the right, and keep going. Look at how experienced recreational skaters do it. Check how graceful and fluid the movement becomes, with each push-off flowing into the next. Do not follow the example of aggressive skaters who have a far more staccato style aimed at maximum acceleration before they go into a trick. You are trying to achieve a non-stop fluid movement.

HEEL BRAKE

Stopping is a critical skill. The basic starter method is to use the heel brake which is fitted to most skates. For it to work, you must be in the proper skating stance, with your centre of gravity over the top of your skates.

Feeling stable enough to try it? OK! Extend your braking skate forwards (most prefer the right foot) and start to pull up on your toes and press down on the heel while pushing down with your body. This will slow you down to an eventual full stop. It will NOT bring you to an immediate stop, and is more about controlled deceleration.

T-STOP

The T-stop is the skater's second method for slowing down, and is essential for skaters who choose to skate without brakes (not recommended for beginners). The technique is to put your skates in a T-position, with the back skate dragging along sideways which slows you down. To do this, you need to balance about 60 per cent of your weight on the front skate, with the remaining 40 per cent on the back skate.

The only way you can master T-stops is if you are confident enough to stay balanced, gliding on the front skate with the back skate lifted, and can then lift the back skate round and lower it so all four wheels kiss the ground together. If you get it a little wrong and the wheels don't touch down evenly or don't form a proper 90-degree T, the usual result is a 'spin stop' which spins you round on the back skate. Even that is quite a good way of stopping. *N.B. One big disadvantage to the T-stop is that it does no favours to the rate of wear on the insides of your braking wheels.*

POWER SLIDE

The power slide is a stopping technique which brings you to a complete stop when travelling at speed. It is useful in an emergency but takes up space, and you need to be skating confidently and

have successfully worked through the heel brake and T-stop before you attempt it.

The technique requires a violent, dynamic movement which is a power-driven extension of the T-stop. The skater turns the right skate while balancing firmly on the left leg which is bent at the knee, and extends the right leg completely so the blade on the skate is at about 45 degrees to the ground. This will bring you to a skidding halt, but the pay-off is very high wear on the insides of your wheels. It's a movement which takes total commitment and self-confidence to perform. No bottling out here!

CROSS-OVER

The cross-over is a more fluid form of skating which allows you to change direction while keeping the power full-on. The technique is to cross the outside skate over the front of the inside skate as you lean into the turn, leaving space to push off with the inside skate. Keep crossing over and pushing off all the way through the turn, and don't trip yourself in the process!

TURNING

Turning on skates is so simple, particularly if you can do it on skis. To turn to the right, just push a little onto the inside edge of your left skate and the outside edge of your right skate. Point your toes and hips in the direction of the turn, and your body will follow. The harder you push, the faster and tighter you will turn. It is a very similar movement to the parallel turn on snow – the main difference is that it is much easier to execute a series of fluid, slalom-style turns!

SURFING

The 'surfing' stance is used by more accomplished skaters to combine elements of snowboarding and skateboarding with inlining. It is a smart move which allows you to turn really easily, jump on your skates, power slide and even get downhill at incredible speeds! It is only for experienced skaters to try.

Want to turn easily? Just switch to surfing! You can maybe combine it with skating backwards, crossing steps and inverting the direction.

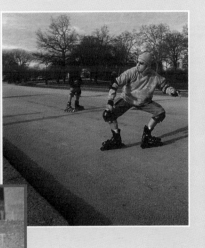

Want to jump a little obstacle like a kerb? Try it the surfing way, with a cool hop-up on the front skate and the back skate following.

SKATE WISE

- ◆ *Stay alert and be courteous at all times.*
- ◆ *Know how to stop. Control your speed. Know how to turn. Learn the basic manoeuvres.*
- ◆ *Keep to the left. Overtake on the right. Indicate direction when passing pedestrians.*
- ◆ *Give pedestrians priority when skating on pavements and footpaths.*
- ◆ *Wear safety equipment at all times including wrist guards, knee and elbow pads. Wearing a helmet is a wise precaution.*
- ◆ *Watch out for obstacles such as uneven and broken tarmac or paving stones, water, oil and anything unpleasant that dogs may have left behind (blame the owner – not the dog). If you can't avoid something, you may trip (or slide) and fall.*
- ◆ *Avoid all areas containing motorized traffic.*

SKATING BACKWARDS

Skating backwards always looks good and draws a crowd of admirers. To get going, push outwards with your left skate, keeping 60 per cent of your weight over the right skate. Let yourself glide backwards with full weight on your right skate, circling your left skate in front to start the sequence rolling again. Don't forget to check behind!

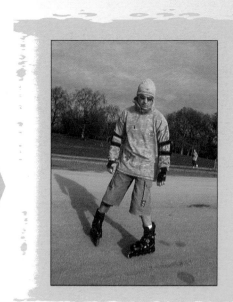

THE GRAPE VINE

The grape vine is all about 100 per cent fun. It is built around skating in a straight line, but as you skate along, you alternate between skating forwards and backwards – and it's no more difficult than crossing your legs!

Start with open legs, then circle your right skate behind the left one to give a half spin of 180 degrees. This gets you skating backwards. Then circle your right skate in front of your left one, and still moving backwards – the trick starts to get difficult here – move your left skate in front of your right skate, spin through another 180 degrees, and find you are skating forwards. The first grape vine is complete, so you are ready to start all over again!

BARREL ROLL

The barrel roll is a skilful trick which allows you to dance to any kind of beat. It's all about skating round in a circle, while spinning at the same time.

Start with your right skate going forwards and your left skate lifted off the ground. The left skate drops onto the ground, and automatically you are skating backwards and starting a circle.

Keep going backwards with the right skate lifted, and as soon as the right skate touches ground lift the left skate which automatically switches you into skating forwards once again. When the circle is completed with a full spin, start the sequence rolling again.

Great Skate Places

With so many skate places to choose from, we can only feature a very small selection. Here are some of the best known on both sides of the Atlantic...

LONDON

Most recreational skating in Central London takes place in Hyde Park. The skate areas are clearly identified, with a lively skate scene stretching from the western end of the park at Kensington Gardens through to the east end of the Serpentine where there are large gatherings of skaters. The closed-off road near the Albert Memorial is a popular spot for pick-up hockey and impromptu slalom.

Elsewhere the recreational skate scene is not so good, because of an almost total ban on skating in London's Royal Parks. These include Primrose Hill, Regent's (unless you skate before 8am!), Holland, Green, St James's, Bushy, Greenwich and Richmond Park. Elsewhere there is limited skate access to Battersea, Victoria, Queens, Finsbury and Clissold Park, plus a lively skate scene at Trafalgar Square which mainly takes place on fine summer evenings.

FLORIDA

Florida is a great place to skate and an outstanding one if you are a beginner. Along with its South Beach, Miami is heavenly for inliners. Everyone is on skates there, and there are endless good places to take part in an area where skating is so readily accepted as an alternative mode of transport that people skate to and from the office. Other top Florida locations include Daytona Beach, Fort Lauderdale and Tampa. June and July are the busy season in Florida; it gets too hot in August, but the long, dry winters are great for skaters. There are plenty of skate shops all over the area with skate equipment often considerably cheaper than Europe.

NEW YORK

The main area for New York recreational skaters is Central Park in the middle of Manhattan, where the through-roads are closed to traffic at weekends so skaters can take over en masse. All ages and abilities are welcomed, from extended families on skates right through to turbo-charged fitness skaters blasting round the road circuit.

Another popular Manhattan spot is the Henry Hudson Parkway, a stretch of promenade along the Hudson River. This is a more laid-back skate area which appeals to sociable skaters in the twenty-something and thirty-something age bracket who form groups along the Parkway on fine evenings. And while you're in Manhattan, check out the Riverside Skate Park, the area's very own aggressive skate park at 108th Street on the west side.

CALIFORNIA

Venice Beach and Santa Monica Beach in Los Angeles are sometimes called the 'Mecca' of inline skating. A twin-lane combined cycle and skate track stretches for miles by the side of the ocean, and is heavily used by skaters of all kinds from recreational, through fitness and hockey. Skate shops and skate hire are on site at most of the main car parks along the way.

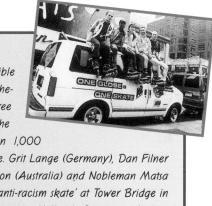

ONE GLOBE — ONE SKATE

One Globe — One Skate (OGOS) was an incredible 10,000 kilometre-long (6,200 mile) round-the-world skate which took place over more than three months in 1997. The five skaters who formed the OGOS Team were selected from more than 1,000 applicants by the Sports University of Cologne. Grit Lange (Germany), Dan Filner (USA), Akhiro Sawauchi (Japan), Mark Gibson (Australia) and Nobleman Matsa (South Africa) started their marathon 'world anti-racism skate' at Tower Bridge in London, and from there skated across Europe via Holland, Germany, Austria, Switzerland, Italy, France and Spain. From there they crossed the Atlantic to skate up through the USA and Canada, before visiting Malaysia, Singapore, Japan and Australia, moving on to South Africa to meet their patron Nelson Mandela, and finally returning to Europe to finish at the Brandenburg Gate in Berlin.

Speed Skating

Competitive speed skating is a racing discipline which takes fitness skating to its extreme conclusion, marrying the skill of skates with the thrill of racing round a track. Speed, tactics and supreme fitness are what counts in the upper levels of a sport which demands nerves of steel, as closely bunched racers hurtle round a course in tightly knit lines, waiting for the moment to spring out of the slipstream and make the finishing sprint for the line. But speed is not all about champions. Like recreational skating, the chance to experience speed is available to skaters of almost any age or ability, with 'rat races' being run for fun for everyone at all big speed events…

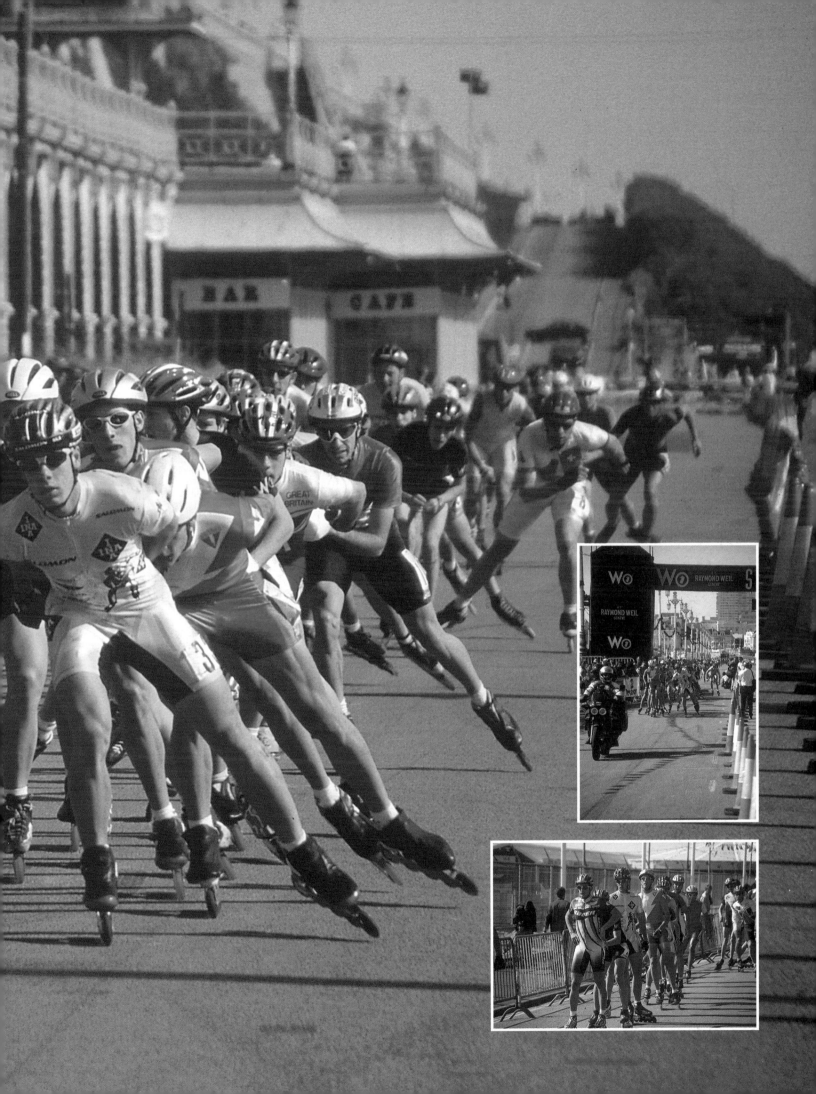

Speed Essentials

'ROLLER SPEED'

The British Federation of Roller Speed (BFRS), known as 'Roller Speed', is the long-established governing body of speed skating in the UK. It manages an annual calendar that ranges from local club racing on tracks throughout the summer to mass-participation events on closed public roads such as the Coventry Marathon. At the top of the scale, it holds international Grand Prix events of various lengths for dedicated speed racers, while recreational and fitness skaters of all ages and abilities are welcome to try the 'Rat Races' which are put on at race meetings by clubs affiliated to Roller Speed.

Rat racing is designed as entry-level racing which gives participants an opportunity to have a go at distance and speed skating in a safe, controlled environment, with plenty of time to get tips from seasoned racers. It also gives them a chance to experience the unique thrill of speed skating round a banked track, such as the purpose-built 200 metre-long Roller Speed track at The Wheels Project in Bordsley Green, Birmingham.

SPECIAL SPEED GEAR

Crash hats

In a sport where speeds can hit 40mph (64km)and skaters are densely packed, the most fundamental item of safety equipment is a crash hat. Any good quality cycle-style crash hat will do, with light weight and good ventilation being at a premium. No top-class speed skater would dream of training without a crash hat, and when it comes to racing, the rule from international championships to first-time racers is 'No Crash Hat, No Race'. Most top racers even put their hats on before they put their skates on.

Guards and pads

The second most important items of protective equipment are wrist guards. In a race most fallers tumble forwards and put their hands down first. The potential broken or sprained wrists plus gravel burns on the palms are prevented by wrist guards. They are easily put on and taken off and do not hinder a racer's style, although some top-class racers opt to do without them.

Knee pads are strongly recommended for all newcomers to racing. If you fall, your hands will generally touch down first with your knees following, but elbows are unlikely to hit the ground which makes elbow guards less essential. Too much safety equipment and you can end up looking like the 'Michelin Man'. Top-class speed skaters wear no pads at all, since they tend to restrict movement and add extra wind drag.

▷ *A wide choice of wheels sets speed skaters apart!*

Skates and wheels

Standard recreational skates with four wheel set-ups of around 76mm size are fine for newcomers to racing. Aggressive skates are less suitable, since small diameter wheels mean you have to work very hard to go fast.

For distance skating and fitness, the bigger the wheels; the better you will go. The minimum size for any event over 500 metres is 78mm, with 80mm being first choice. A five wheel set-up is better than four since it provides a longer base with a smoother ride, more power in the push and more glide in the recovery from each push.

The rule of thumb when selecting wheels is soft on rough surfaces and hard on very smooth surfaces, but the harder the wheel, and the smoother the surface, the more slip you get with each push. Try 76A (soft) for very rough, 80A for general purpose and 84A (hard) for very smooth. Remember that what suits a 30kg man may not suit a 15kg lady, and speed is to do with personal preferences – some skaters like plenty of grip while others prefer to feel a little slide.

For racing and race-training, serious skaters will have at least two sets of general purpose wheels, plus one set of soft and one of hard wheels for specific uses. Make regular checks, look for wear on the wheels, turn them and move their position in the chassis. Do not skate on badly worn wheels which can be a danger to you and other racers.

▽ *Training for distance makes speed skating a tough and dedicated sport for top athletes.*

Speed bearings

Top ABEC and Swiss bearings are best, since the smoother the bearings run, the better you will go and the less energy you need expend to skate fast. You must also take care of them. Training for the serious skater takes place in all weathers, and water and dust are the two great enemies of smooth-running bearings.

After a wet skate, strip and dry the boots and chassis, take the bearings out, clean them in a water-repellent, let them dry, make sure they run free, and give them a light coating of lubricant such as WD40, GT95 or similar. After a long, dry skate in summer, make sure the bearings are free from dust which can get in amongst the bearings and scours and wears them down. Watch out for badly worn bearings which may collapse at high speed, leading to a potentially dangerous wipe-out.

Ultimate speed skates

For serious fitness and distance skaters the optimum skate has five large-diameter wheels of around 80mm mounted in a lightweight aluminium chassis with comfortable, low-cut leather boots with a flush-fitting axle system that makes it quick and easy to change or rotate wheels which suffer a lot of wear in training or racing. At top level you could expect to pay serious money (which may exceed £1,000) for a pair of top racing skates. Reckon on around £200 for the aluminium chassis, plus ultra stiff carbon-fibre-soled boots ranging from £200 off the shelf to £700 and more for the ultimate made-to-measure models, plus each set of 10 wheels costing £100 or more if they are top quality and 20 speed bearings adding another £120!

▷ *Speed action during a marathon race in Brighton.*

Speed Disciplines

RACE EVENTS

Speed events are generally divided between 'Fun Races' or 'Rat Races' which are open to all with no particular speed skills, and the dedicated racing disciplines open to Senior (adult men and women), Junior (11-15 year-old boys and girls) and Mini (6-10 year-old boys and girls) classes racing in any of the following events:

Sprints

Short races held over 300, 500 or 1,500 metres from a standing start with groups of up to ten skaters racing to qualify for final heats. Sprints can be held indoors or outdoors, as circuit races round flat or banked tracks, or on straight-line courses. Ippolito Sanfratello of Italy was the 1997 300 Metre World Champion, and was hailed as 'the world's fastest man on skates' after taking just 24.4 seconds to cover the distance.

Mid-distance races

Usually held over 5,000 metres or 10,000 metres. This event combines elements of endurance and sprint skating using a track or closed road circuit. Arnaud Gicquel of France was the 1997 10,000 Metre World Champion.

Marathon races

Traditionally held over 26.2 miles or 50 kilometres on a track or closed road circuit. 20,000 metres can be used as a half-marathon distance. In the annual Coventry City Marathon, this event takes place over three laps of the inner city ring road. Massimilio Presti of Italy was the 1997 World Marathon Champion.

Endurance races

Held over any reasonable length, with 100 miles (161km) being a standard long-distance target.

TACTICS & TECHNIQUES

Racing speed is achieved through a combination of fitness and refined technique. Both aspects are the result of training and practice, with programmes such as repeatedly sprinting uphill being used to build up ability. The third aspect of the equation is tactics, employing skills that are in many ways similar to cycle racing.

The pace

How fast you can skate is determined by how fast you can move and push your legs in totally fluid co-ordination. The glide time when your body is balanced over the glide skate between strokes is vital, since it determines the amount of actual rest time for your body. So a long glide is used for endurance, with a short glide combined with sharp, powerful pushes for sprinting and top speed.

The start

The object is to leave the line as fast as possible, pushing off hard without tripping on the skates of another racer. To start fast you take smaller, quicker steps with the skates, leaning forward and bending your knees. Pump your arms hard and fast, and push straight back with each foot turned sideways to initiate the acceleration. After first take-off, start pushing more and more outwards with the skates, lowering your body for stability.

The pace line

With the exception of short sprints, racers will soon form 'pace lines' in which skaters slipstream one another, conserving energy, and taking it in turns to 'make the pace' at the front or take a rest at the back. Skating in a pace line involves skating in a tightly bunched group of people, and is a skill which demands a certain level of experience if the skaters are to stay safely together at speed.

Making a break

Some skaters will drop off the back of a pace line and perhaps join a slower pace line because they cannot hold the speed. Others may want to increase the pace, and will conserve energy while they wait to make a break, taking a few like-minded skaters with them as they accelerate out of line. Once clear, they will reform into their own pace line which is far enough in front of the others to keep moving ahead.

Downhill dangers

Some longer races on open road courses will include downhill sections which tax the racers' skills and nerves to the limits. 'Speed wobble' occurs when gliding on a fast downhill and can make your legs shake so much that you lose control and wipe out. It is solved by actively skating down the hill, pushing with your skates to tighten up the leg muscles and maintain a solid lower frame for your body

The finish

Towards the finish, the pace lines will tend to get faster and more ragged, with skaters breaking out of line and sprinting ahead on their own. A strong skater can make and hold a break well before the line. With skaters of similar ability, the favoured technique is to delay the sprint until the last moments, conserving energy for a gut-bursting rush for the line.

△ *Downhill madness at Lausanne! The racers risk everything in this downhill speed classic.*

Aggressive Skating

Aggressive skaters are the image-makers who help define inline skating today. These are young skaters who have moved the sport in an exciting, dynamic, ever-changing direction which demands guts and honesty as the stakes are piled ever higher. They divide into 'vert' skaters and 'street' skaters, with the vert specialists skating high in the sky off the big half pipe ramp while street exponents fly off and 'grind' on any suitable surface, whether purpose-built in a skate park or in a real street environment. Both elements of aggressive skating are responding to a three-headed challenge: to push the limits of technique, gymnastic ability and danger…

Aggressive Equipment

HELMETS

There are plenty of skate helmets available, and the choice has been made simpler by the introduction of the new CE EN 1078 standard in 1998. This is designed to dispel confusion and ensure that only helmets which actually protect the skull by absorbing impact are sold to inline skaters. To achieve this CE EN 1078 requires:

◆ Impact absorption tests conducted to simulate falls on a flat surface from 1.5 metres.
◆ Impact absorption tests conducted to simulate falls on a sharp edge from 1.1 metres.
◆ Retention system tests (revealing how well the straps work) .

All helmets which offer proper protection for skaters should now conform to the EN1078 Standard which is clearly shown by a label. Even this is no guarantee as to a helmet's safety, however, since CE EN 1078 is a general standard which applies to cycling and skateboarding as well as inline skating, and each discipline has rather different requirements – a cycling helmet is designed to withstand a single major impact after which it should be thrown away,

◁ *A helmet should be comfortable, secure, fit tightly and conform to European standards.*

while an aggressive skating helmet is more likely to need to handle lots of small knocks.

It is vital that a helmet fits properly, is comfortable, and is done up securely so the strap is tight enough to keep it on without restricting breathing. Aim for a helmet with a perfect fit, using different-thickness removable foam pads as necessary. Test the weight, which varies greatly between some brands. Also consider ventilation, which is a high priority in warm weather and indoor environments.

SKATE SAFE
◆ *Always wear protective equipment and skate within your capabilities.*
◆ *Beware of all traffic.*
◆ *Skate to give skating a good name!*

AGGRESSIVE EXTRAS

Crash Shorts
Fully padded shorts provide protection round the hips and at the base of the spine.

Grind Plates
Reinforcing plate which bolts to the inside of the chassis for grinding between the middle two wheels. Plastic grind plates are favoured for a controlled, slower ride. Aluminium grind plates have less friction and give a much faster ride, and are only suitable for experts. Grind plates can be replaced on all skates.

H-Blocks
Removable H-shaped block which fits inside the chassis and gives extra support between the middle two wheels when grinding. H-blocks can be replaced on all skates.

Shin Guards
Extra protection for the vulnerable area between knee pads and skates when skating on ramps and practising extreme street skating.

Skate Jeans
Cut wide and baggy from the knee to accommodate knee pads and shin pads with a flare to drop over the top of the skates and plenty of reinforcement. Can incorporate removable padding to protect hips and base of the spine.

Skate Paints
Scratch and chip-free paint applicators used to decorate faded skates and wheels.

Soul Plates
Reinforcing plate for soul (sole) area on the outside of each boot. Used for grinding along the full length of the skate on kerbs or rails. Soul plates can be replaced on some skates.

GRIND WAX

Grind wax is used for preparing pavement kerbs, steps and other urban surfaces for a smooth ride while grinding between the middle two wheels. Branded wax with names such as Sex Wax and Slam Butter can be bought over the counter in a skate shop, but many skaters prefer to experiment by making their own concoctions.

△ *Wax provides a smooth surface for skates to slide along.*

Making wax

Skaters swear by their own wax recipes which often feature an outlandish list of ingredients. Whatever you do, you must ask permission before you borrow things from someone else's kitchen, be careful to clear up your mess, and don't burn down the house in the process!

Here is a typical grind wax recipe in which almost anything goes:

1. Get an old saucepan and a wooden spoon which you can use exclusively for making wax.
2. Put in four candles with the wicks removed. Coloured candles will help colour the wax, or you can add your favourite colour by crumbling in wax crayons.
3. Set the pan over a low heat and use the wooden spoon to stir in four squirts of washing-up liquid (some disagree on this), four lard balls, four butter blobs, two bath balls and two tablespoons of grease.
4. When the mixture is melted and well mixed, use a funnel to pour it into an empty plastic drinks bottle – not too hot, or you could melt the plastic. Some like to insert a stick in the neck, so the hard wax can eventually be handled like a lolly.
5. Put the bottle in the fridge or freezer, and leave until the wax is set firm.
6. Take out the bottle, and cut off the plastic bottom so the wax block can be removed.
7. Your grind wax is now ready for use.

Applying the wax

There are a number of methods for applying wax, based on personal trial and error. Try this for a fast, smooth grinding surface:

1. Find the longest, smoothest concrete kerbs possible.
2. Fill any gaps between the kerb stones with wax, using a cigarette lighter to melt and mould it to shape.
3. Lightly rub the main grinding area where the chassis will slide with a bar of wax.
4. Rub a bar of soap on top of the wax and leave to dry.
5. Rub on a final top layer of wax.

△ *Grindplates and grind wax go together, allowing the chassis to slide sideways.*

Get A Skate Park

Many aggressive skaters are frustrated by the lack of places to skate. In public locations they are often regarded as a menace, performing their tricks on hand-rails, stairs and kerbs which eventually get damaged, and getting in the way of cars on the streets and in car parks, sometimes with tragic consequences.

The answer is that it's safer and more socially acceptable to get off the street. To do this, aggressive skaters need skate parks which provide all the facilities they want in a safe and secure environment. If you are lucky enough to live in a place like Florida, skate parks can be found out of doors, but for Britain and most of Europe indoor skate parks are required as well.

In the past few years of the skate boom, plenty of new skate parks have been opened in the UK, many with local government assistance and funding. There are still plenty of holes in the UK skate-park map, and a lot more parks will be needed to satisfy growing demand. The problem is to persuade local authorities and businessmen that they are both viable and necessary, and a carefully managed campaign is the only way to get results.

Why does your area need a skate park?

1. A permanent skate park provides a social and recreational focus for young people whose only alternative is to skate on the streets.
2. Without such a focal point, some young people will turn to crime.
3. When aggressive skaters take to the streets, it can involve unintentional and innocent vandalism to property and danger to pedestrians, but there may be no alternative place to skate.
4. A skate park can help to educate and influence the behaviour of young people. It can allow them to take more control of their sportand learn to respect their environment.

▷ *An open-air skate park is great for summer use, but may virtually close down in winter.*

△ *An indoor park provides a year-round environment. This is 'Vertical' near London Airport.*

Who would use a skate park?

A comprehensive and authoritative survey of local skaters is an important marketing tool for establishing the need for a skate park. The survey could take the form of a questionnaire combined with a petition, circulated via skate shops, schools and other sympathetic outlets.

The survey should establish:
◆ The age range of skaters.
◆ The gender of skaters.
◆ How long they have been skating.
◆ How they like to skate.
◆ What facilities they expect at a skate park.
◆ How far they are prepared or able to travel to a skate park.
◆ How much they can pay to use a skate park.
◆ How often they would use a skate park.
◆ Preference for an indoor or outdoor skate park.

SETTING GOALS

What is the target?

To establish a long-term skate park. Note that many local authorities built parks to cope with the skateboard boom in the 1970s. When skateboarding went out of fashion, the skate parks fell into disuse and became expensive white elephants. Local authorities must be persuaded that they are not making the same mistake again.

What type of skate park do we need?

◆ Outdoor skate parks are often local owned by the authority and offer free use for skaters. While sites can be easy to find, they require major funding for weather-proof construction followed by minor funding for maintenance. There may be objections to an unsupervised facility that is open to potential litigation from injured parties, and lack of use due to poor weather conditions.

◆ Indoor skate parks need to charge for their facilities due to their much higher running costs. With the costs of commercial property too high to be a realistic option, the most likely facility could be a disused warehouse or similar large building which is provided by the local authority for a commercial management.

What scale is required?

A minimum of 15,000 square feet (1,4000m^2)would allow for:

◆ A smooth, hard area fitted with street-style obstacles and mini ramps.
◆ A large area fitted with bowls and more advanced ramps for the better skaters.
◆ Extra space for skateboards, BMX or hockey which could help fund the project.
◆ Adequate spectator space.

What amenities are required?

All skaters should be able to make positive and productive use of the facility and feel welcome there. Desirable amenities should include:

◆ Workshop and office.
◆ Car parking area.
◆ Toilet, changing room and showers.
◆ Hire and equipment shop.
◆ Rest area and games room.
◆ Cafe/restaurant.
◆ First Aid facility.

What location is required?

This can be a major problem. Important factors might include easy access by public transport, a safe route and secure parking for bicycles, adequate on-site parking, and – if possible – a location which is in an attractive, people-friendly area which includes shops, cafes and other recreational facilities.

GETTING THE WHEELS ROLLING

1. Form a Skate Supporters Association with a steering committee to spearhead the campaign, raise public awareness of the need for a skate park, and attract interested parties. Work with skateboarders, BMX'ers and hockey players if their needs fit in with your requirements.

2. Produce an authoritative survey combined with a petition which represents the views of a large cross-section of skaters.

3. Produce a clearly argued report to present ideas and initial estimates of likely size, scale of amenities, indoor or outdoor location and accessibility.

4. Seek assistance in locating a suitable site for the skate park via local authorities, commercial surveyors, private landowners and businesses.

5. Find an accountant or other professional to advise on a bid for major funding, and to assist in budgeting.

6. Identify local authorities, charities and businesses which might be prepared to contribute to a fighting fund.

7. Find an architect who will prepare sketch plans of the project.

8. Employ the architect to act as planning consultant and prepare a planning application for the local authority.

Skate Park Elements

Skate parks have a variety of elements or obstacles divided between 'Street', which includes all the elements of grinding, drop-ins, fly-offs, flips and other tricks on ramps and rails, and pure 'Vert' which takes place on a full-size 'half pipe'. For indoor use the principal construction material for the ramps is typically plywood sheets of less than half an inch (12mm) thickness, laid in multiple layers and supported on a rigid, cross-braced wooden frame.

Rails and kerbs

Rails and kerbs are major elements in a street course which may feature round rails, box-shape rails ('planters') and kinked rails, plus kerbs (marble is the toughest, smoothest material) for grinds.

Pyramid

Square box with flat ramps forming the sides which looks like a pyramid. The pointed top is usually cut off for safety reasons, with the flat area being good for flying 'airs' over the top.

Death box

A bigger box designed to generate high airs. The skater hits the steep transition at speed, takes off, and rolls out smoothly and safely on the flat bank on the other side.

Flat bank

The simplest type of ramp. It comprises a flat ramp set against a vertical surface.

Driveway

A box with flat banks both sides plus a planter.

Fun box

Multi-obstacle box incorporating rails, planters, transitions and flat banks. Typical set-up could include a platform about three feet (1m) high, with a grind box on top featuring double coping. You can skate the box from both sides, forward or back, since the wedges and rails are absolutely symmetrical.

Mini ramp

A small half pipe with a curved drop which is about three to six feet (1 to 1.8m) high and has no element of vert. This makes it suitable for lip tricks and flips, but not for airs, as the skater will drift away from the ramp while flying. A mini can have a flat deck or narrow 'spine' when ramps are set back-to-back to look like a 'W'. A bigger mini ramp becomes a 'midi' ramp while a smaller mini is a 'micro'.

Quarter pipe

Small curved ramp which approximates to a quarter of a round pipe and may have an element of 'vert' (when the top of the curve ends with a short vertical section) for performing airs. Typical radius is up to about six feet (1.8m) high, with a ten feet (3m) deep 'transition' area where the skaters drop in, fly off and turn. The top of the ramp can be fitted with PVC or steel coping for grinding.

A quarter pipe can be used as a launch ramp off a flat deck to give the skater fast acceleration when dropping in for a trick routine on various obstacles, or a sequence of quarter pipes with different gradients can be laid out to make up a run with flat platforms and back-to-back double coping.

Half pipe

Monster twin ramp which approximates to half of a round pipe when seen from the side, though it doesn't really look like it as it has a wide expanse of 'flat' in between. Maximum height up to about 11.5ft (3.5m), with the two facing transitions having up to 20in (50cm) of 'vert' at the top of each ramp. This allows air tricks where the skaters can launch and land without drifting away from the ramp. Transitions are performed on the 'coping', a PVC or steel pipe that runs along the front of the top of the ramp, though 'elevators' may include a vertical section above the coping. Each side has a horizontal deck where the skaters wait their turns to drop in or roll out. Two half pipes can be mounted in sequence as 'spine ramps' in the shape of a monster 'W'

Typical dimensions for a full half pipe could be:

◆ Overall length – 46ft (14m)
◆ Overall width – 16.5ft (5m)
◆ Area of flat between transitions – 16.5ft (5m)
◆ Two transitions – 10ft (3m)
◆ Two drop-in and roll-out decks – 5ft (1.5m)
◆ Vertical height – 11.5ft (3.5m)

Full pipe

Very unusual – a complete pipe which goes all the way round. The only way to enter it is at speed, with the aid of a 'snake run' which lets the skater accelerate madly down from a high, narrow slalom which is like a toboggan run and about 80ft (25m) long. Not for the faint hearted!

HOME EQUIPMENT

Aggressive equipment, such as grind poles and fun boxes, are commercially available for use on a small scale, with applications for local groups, school playgrounds or a well-endowed home. Typical examples are the grind pole and fun box shown here, both manufactured by Pro Move Equipment.

△ *The grind pole is designed for year-round outdoor use, and features a ten feet (3m) long galvanized mild steel pole with a 1.75in (44mm) diameter, mounted on detachable legs for easy storage. The manufacturer claims it is stable and will not slide on tarmac or concrete, which is obviously of vital importance.*

△ *The fun box is supplied as a flat-pack so it can be stored in inclement weather, and features ramps and deck made of exterior grade ply mounted on a 24in (60cm) high mild steel frame with the option of a ten feet (3m) grind pole.*

Bowls

Landscape bowls moulded in concrete are mostly found in outdoor skate parks which date back to skateboarding times, with flowing designs that were originally modelled on Californian swimming pools. At its simplest the bowl is simply a rounded hole scooped into the ground, but most include changes in gradient and direction plus a 'hip' which lets the skater take off and land on the sides of the bowl. If you image a Valentine's heart-shaped bowl, the hip would be formed where the curves of the heart slope in and join at the top.

Make your own

For the budget-conscious, it is relatively easy to transform a builders' scaffolding pipe into a usable grind pole for basic training. All you need to do is find a means of securing it safely. If you feel capable of a more advanced level of design and construction, you could try your skills at something more enterprising which allows more grind variations. As an example, a simple, rigid plywood box with carrying handles, fitted with heavy-duty plastic grind poles bolted to the top of each side, becomes a twin-railed skate box with minimum expense and a little ingenuity..

Kinds of Grinds

1. SOUL
Sliding forwards =
Soul Grind.
Sliding backwards =
Alley-Oop Soul.

3. MAKIO
Sliding forwards =
Makio.
Sliding backwards =
Alley-Oop Makio.

2. ACID
Sliding forwards =
Acid Soul.
Sliding backwards =
Alley-Oop Acid.

4. ROCKET GRAB MAKIO
Sliding forwards =
Rocket Makio.
Sliding backwards =
Alley-Oop Rocket
Makio.

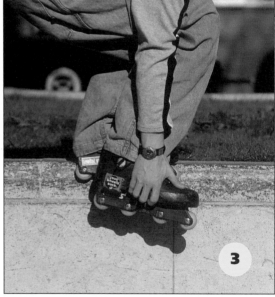

5. MIZOU

Sliding forwards = Mizou. Sliding backwards = Alley-Oop Mizou.

6. PORNSTAR

Sliding backwards = Acid Mizou.
Sliding forwards = Pornstar forwards.
Sliding forwards topside = Sunny Day.
Sliding backwards topside = Topside Pornstar.

7. 50 PER CENT

Sliding forwards = 50 Per Cent.
Sliding backwards = Alley-Oop 50 Per Cent.

8. SIDEWALK

Sliding forwards = Sidewalk. Sliding backwards = Alley-Oop Sidewalk.

9. TOPSIDE SOUL

Sliding forwards = Topside Soul. Sliding backwards = Alley-Oop Topside Soul.

10. UFO

Sliding frontside = UFO.
Sliding backside =
Backside UFO.

11. TOPSIDE ACID

Sliding forwards =
Topside Acid.
Sliding backwards =
Alley-Oop Topside Acid.

12. FISHBONE

Sliding forwards =
Fishbone.
Sliding backwards =
Alley-Oop Fishbone.

13. FISHBRAIN

Sliding forwards =
Fishbrain.
Sliding backwards =
Alley-Oop Fishbrain.

14. ROYALE   15. BACKSIDE ROYALE

16. TORQUE SOUL

17. TOPSIDE TORQUE SOUL

18. TORQUE SLIDE
Sliding forwards = Torque Slide.

19. UNITY
Sliding frontside = Unity.
Sliding backside = Backside Unity.

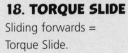

GRIND GLOSSARY

FRONTSIDE = Facing inwards – e.g. on a kerb with your front to the pavement.

BACKSIDE = Facing outwards – e.g. on a kerb with your back to the pavement, grinding 'arse first'.

TOPSIDE = Laying the soul area flat on the grinding surface so the blade is boned-over at 90 degrees.

BONE-OVER = Bending your legs over to the limit.

20. TRAINING WHEEL

Sliding forwards = Training Wheel.
Sliding backwards = Alley-Oop Training Wheel.

21. TRAINING WHEEL TOPSIDE

Sliding forwards = Training Wheel Topside.
Sliding backwards = Alley-Oop Training Wheel Topside.

22. BACKSLIDE

Sliding backwards frontside = Frontside Backslide.
Sliding backwards backside = Backside Backslide.

23. NINE BAR

24. WHEEL BARROW

25. SWEAT STANCE/KIND GRIND

Sweat Stance forwards = Kind Grind backwards.

26. DUST BUSTER

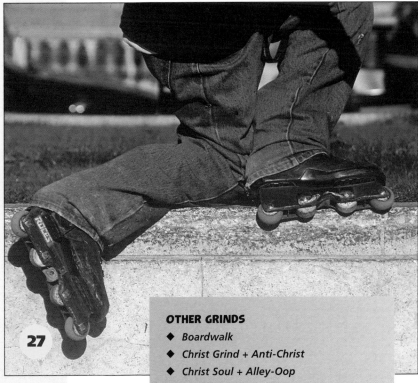

27. TENDANT TEAR

OTHER GRINDS

◆ *Boardwalk*

◆ *Christ Grind + Anti-Christ*

◆ *Christ Soul + Alley-Oop*

◆ *Christ Topside + Alley-Oop*

◆ *Fahrvegnügen*

◆ *Fahrvegnügen Christ*

◆ *Cab Driver*

◆ *Side Surf Grind*

... and many more great grinds to come!

28. STUB GRIND

Airs & Grinds

Over to Matt King and Ryan Wood to give a demonstration of some of the many airs and grinds that can be performed using the ramps at an indoor or outdoor skate park. Just remember that it takes many hours of practice to get to this kind of level, and full safety gear must be worn at all times...

Japan Air

Ryan Wood transfers from the quarter pipe to the flat bank with a 180 degree spin.

AIRS can be performed on both ramps and street. Doing a grab whilst 'catching air' makes these manoeuvres both fun and stylish. Whilst airborne the skater can perform spins, flips and grabs, or a combination of all three, while in competitions more points are awarded for height and variation.

Mute Air 360

Ryan Wood transfers from the quarter pipe to the flat bank using a mute air combined with a 360 degree spin.

Stale Japan

Matt King uses a Stale Japan to transfer from the quarter pipe to the flat bank with a 180 degree spin.

GRINDS originated on the street, using hand rails and ledges, but can also be performed on the metal coping of a ramp. There are many different types of grinds and even more grind variations, like 'Switches' which involve changing feet on the rail. In competitions more points are scored for longer, smoother grinds.

Frontside

Matt King performs one of the oldest grinds in rollerblading. Legs are spread wide apart, grinding on the inside edges between the two centre wheels of each skate.

Royale

Matt King shows off the Royale, which is like a Frontside, but with the trailing foot 'boned over' (pushed hard over) onto the outside edge of the boot.

Soul Grind

This is one of the oldest, most used, and most stylish grinds in rollerblading. Weight is placed on the soul of the back foot, with the leading foot extended out in front as shown here by Matt King.

Matt King – Royale

Parallel Grab

One of the harder grabs in rollerblading. The hand reaches over the top of the knee to grab the opposite boot.

Kung Lao

When you get air off the ramp, the kicked out foot should be facing the sky as you grab the inside boot. Either your right hand grabs the the right boot, or your left hand grabs the left boot.

Rocket Air

Both legs are extended out in front of the body – right hand to left toe, left hand to right toe. A variation on this move is a 'Cross Rocket' when the skater crosses his legs while doing the grab.

Mute Air

Matt King reaches his right hand over both shins to grab his left foot. The Mute Air is one of the oldest and most used airs in rollerblading.

Fly Fish

Matt King shows off a Fly Fish, one of the newest grabs in rollerblading. The right hand grabs the right boot and extends the leg, while the left foot is tucked under the body.

▷ *Matt King – Japan Air*

Stale Japan Air

Matt King demonstrates the meaning of the word 'Stale' which is all about grabbing a foot from behind.

Safety Grab

Matt King shows a fundamental move in ramp skating – right hand on right boot or left hand on left boot, with knees tucked up so the skater is in a ball.

Method Air

Both legs are pulled back behind the body in this trick by Matt King. The right hand grabs the left boot or the left hand grabs the right boot.

Matt King – Safety Grab

Cab Bio 540

This combined spin and flip is approached backwards up the ramp – ie 'Cab'.
It is a 540 degree spin with the body angled to the side as shown by Matt King.

Big Events / Halls of Fame

INTERNATIONAL COMPETITION

The National Inline Skate Series (NISS) is the original big skate tour, created by Rick Stark and Mark Billik of Anywhere Sport Productions in 1994 when it took off with TV coverage. NISS now travels 10,000 miles across the states of the USA to visit 10 three day weekend events held between May and September, with a 16 strong support team transporting and setting up some 30,000 pounds of ramps, tents and equipment that are necessary for the tour.

▷ *Pro skaters go to the limits at IISS and ASA competitions and events like the 'Pipe Tribe' in Dortmund.*

▷ *Thiag Khris won the 'Vert' competition at the IISS Finals in 1997, and is widely regarded as one of the greatest skaters the sport has produced. This is him in action at Lausanne.*

IISS & ASA

The International Inline Skate Series (IISS) was a direct development of NISS, run on the same style by Anywhere Sports Productions at major three day venues around the world. The 1997 series was held at venues in Brazil, Australia, Germany and Spain, culminating in the International Finals at Amsterdam in Holland in December, acknowledged as the world's number indoor event.

A rival body known as the Aggressive Skaters Association (ASA) was also established, running an ASA World Tour based on events such as the X-Trials in Orlando, California which is solely open to the top professional skaters.

With radical new moves such as the McTwist and Rocket first seen on the NISS tour, it has been the proving ground for top skaters such as Chris Edwards, Tom Fry, Arlo Eisenburg, Randy 'Roadhouse' Spizer and Chris Hines. The men were joined by the women in 1995, when Dawn Everett, Kate Kengo and Ayum Kawasaki first came on the scene, and the best amateur skaters can also try their luck by qualifying to take on the pros. This makes it usual to have 300 or more entries for each NISS event, with 75,000 spectators turning out for the final round of the 1997 series – the US Championships held at Santa Monica, California.

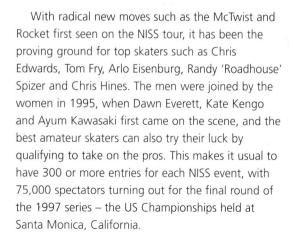

Matt King pauses for a drink while competing at Lousanne. It's thirsty work being a top pro skater!

Disciplines

Thirty or so top pros are automatically pre-qualified for NISS and IISS events through scoring top results, with the rest of the entry having to fight for 16 slots during qualifying rounds held on the first day. The competition is divided between Street and Half Pipe or 'Vert'. In the first year or so of NISS most skaters would enter both disciplines, with skills on Vert starting out similar to Street. However as the sport developed Street and Vert began to move into different directions, and it became normal for skaters to specialise in one or other discipline.

Street is combination of transitions and rails, with NISS and IISS events based around two eight foot quarter pipes serving as a starting point for the course. Once on the course, competitors have a variety of ramps to choose from including the Bauer Box (a half pyramid ramp with a planter), the famous Death Box (a tall fun box with high and low rails for technical tricks), and the two-level 45 degree Hip with an extended coping that curves to the ground for transfers both natural (forward) and alley-oop (backwards). The Street course also includes a Curved Bank for a variety of tricks, plus two smaller launch ramps for airs and grinding.

The Half Pipe for the Vert skaters is ideally 10 foot 9 inches high and 24 feet wide, which most skaters consider the perfect size for competition use. The radius of the transition area is 9ft 6in, and the vertical section is 1ft 3in. The flat bottom between the transitions is 16ft long, giving skaters enough time and space to set up for their next gravity-defying move. The tops of the transition areas have metal coping for all types of stalls and grinds.

△ ▽ *Thiag Khris hits 2.90 metres above the deck during a 'high air' competition. He won of course...*

◁ *Pro skaters wait for their turns at Lausanne. Britain's Jenny Logue is nearest the camera.*

▽ *BT sponsored the first British team event at the Play Station Skate Park in London.*

Marco Hintze is widely regarded as one of the world's finest competition 'street' skaters.

Judging

After time for a warm-up, each competitor has a 60 second run on the Street course. The time for Vert was reduced from 60 seconds to 50 seconds during the 1997 season, as it is such a physically taxing discipline. Competitors may be allowed two or three runs, with the best or the best average counting. Competitors in both the Street and Vert disciplines are judged on four categories:

Style. *Possibly the most difficult category to judge. The judges look for an individual style which is smooth and solid with a tight body.*

Difficulty. *The judges mark on the difficulty of tricks, as well as how fast the skater gets round the street course and what obstacles the skater is using.*

Consistency. *The judges mark on how the skater keeps moving, and note the number of falls.*

Line. *Line is defined as the route taken by the skater. The judges look for skaters who include the entire course in their Street run, and link tricks and use the half pipe to maximum advantage on the Vert.*

Up to the start of the 1998 season, each category was marked out of 25 points giving a possible total of 100. With the jury made up of seven judges, the lowest and highest score would be dropped from the judges' total in an effort to rule out major discrepancies. However after four years of NISS it was widely felt that the judging system favoured particular skaters who always seemed to emerge on top, even though others appeared just as talented. Part of the problem was down to the equal weighting of the four categories, and ideas being considered included reducing Consistency to 10 (if you fall at that level, it's bad luck) and increasing the scores for Style and Difficulty.

LAUSANNE

The International Inline Festival at Lausanne stands out as the biggest and most stylish aggressive event in Europe. It takes place over three days in August, with a beautiful lakeside setting in the old Swiss city of Lausanne. The main competition is for men and women in Street and Vert with pre-qualified pro skaters fighting off enthusiastic amateurs. There is also a Mini Ramp competition open to all, plus a freakish Downhill Race in which lycra skinsuit competitors hit mad speeds as they tear down through the steep hillside streets of Lausanne.

The whole city is given over to skating during this event which becomes a massive inline celebration, culminating in the famous torchlit parade when an estimated 150,000 skaters roll thorough the town.

The Philips Eargear 1997 UK National Championship was held at the NEC in Birmingham. Here is some action on the 'Street' course...

Hockey Skating

Hockey on inlines is a direct descendant of hockey on ice, which is fitting as inline skates were originally developed for off-ice training. It's a fast-moving, hard-hitting sport in which teams play with an ice-style puck or more conventional ball, and in most types of game the skaters have to wear full protective equipment including visors and body armour to allow for high-speed crashes. To play the game at the top level demands almost perfect skating and stick-handling technique combined with physical endurance and the ability to work as part of a team. However, like most aspects of inline skating, hockey is accessible to all ages and abilities, with the very youngest starting to play as under-10-year-old 'minnows'…

Pick-Up Hockey

The term 'pick-up hockey' originally applied to an informal type of hockey also known as 'street hockey', with few or no rules, which was played outside on any piece of ground smooth enough to skate on. All you needed was a stick, skates, a ball and something in which to score goals. It remains that way today and is the most relaxed form of hockey, while the formal game itself has progressed into a much more sophisticated style of 'off-ice hockey', played indoors on sports courts with balls and pucks and based on the more traditional ice hockey game.

Pick-up rules

The only rules that exist are the ones on which the players agree before the game. Both teams consist of a bunch of people who are playing purely for fun, and you don't even need a goalie when small goals (you build your own) make it difficult to score anyway. However, it is in the players' interests that basic rules are sorted out to minimize disputes and keep the game as safe as possible.

There are a number of popular pick-up rules:

1. When choosing teams, the players turn up and dump their sticks in a pile. Each team captain takes it in turn to pick up a stick, and gets the player who owns the stick each time.

2. When other teams are waiting to play the ground, teams will often play 'first team to two goals wins' and 'winning team stays on'.

3. To prevent dust-ups behind the goal, or the ball being played out of the playing area, there is an understanding that the player with possession of the ball behind the goal line must not be challenged for the ball until it crosses back in front of the goal line.

4. The most important rule is 'You must have fun!'

Pick-up gear

Accidents happen, and falls and crashes are a part of hockey. The level of equipment you need depends on the level of pick-up you play. This can range from a low, easy standard of gently hitting a ball around with young children joining in the game, to top hockey players enjoying the liberating experience of a game of pick-up, but still playing at full energy.

The minimum requirements to enjoy the game are likely to be:

◆ Skates
◆ Stick
◆ Ball (or a puck on suitably smooth non-tarmac surface)
◆ Gloves (optional, but recommended)
◆ Elbow and knee pads (minimum sensible protection from 'gravel rash')
◆ Helmet with visor + full body armour (sensible at the serious end of the game).

Pick-up advantages

◆ A game takes seconds to set-up in a quiet car park or dead-end road.

◆ Minimum gear required – you can play the game with regular recreational or aggressive skates and pads, plus a low-cost wooden stick and a ball.

◆ Easy to understand rules in a relaxed environment – no referee to hassle you!

◆ Playing outdoors – nothing better on a fine summer's day!

◆ Meeting new people and learning skating skills from them.

◆ Fun competition without the pressures and costs of playing hockey at a higher level.

◆ A good game for players of almost any age and ability.

Pick-up disadvantages

◆ Protection is down to you – no first aid or immediate cover is usually available.

◆ Good for progressing to a certain skill level, but beyond that the more serious forms of organized hockey are the way to go in terms of improving technique and meeting a greater challenge.

△ ▷ Set up a small, easily portable goal...

◁ △ ...get together some friends who enjoy skating...

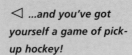

▷ ...issue them with sticks and a ball...

◁ ...and you've got yourself a game of pick-up hockey!

Hockey Equipment

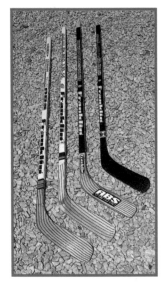

△ Sticks come in all shapes and sizes to give a perfect fit and perfect handling.

CHOOSING STICKS

Sticks come in a variety of materials and sizes, and vary in price from under £10 to over £100. The correct length, 'lie' (the way the blade lies on the ground) and flexibility are important for proper puck and ball control.

Design differences

There are two basic designs of sticks.

◆ The complete stick which is all-in-one.
◆ A shaft joined to a separate blade that can be replaced when worn or broken.

A basic or beginners' stick has a wooden shaft and a plastic blade secured in place with wood screws. The blade is curved so that it can be used by either right- or left-handed players. In addition, Junior sticks with narrower shafts and smaller blades are available for younger players.

All-in-one sticks, both Junior and Senior, usually have a wooden blade and shaft. The shafts and blades are reinforced with glass, epoxy, polyester or kevlar laminates to produce a strong, light and flexible stick.

Shafts that can take separate blades are made from lightweight aluminium or a composite material using advanced fibres. There is a wide selection of blades available to fit these shafts. The blades are usually glued in place, although there are other methods of securing them. Shafts can vary in style, but you must make sure that a new blade fits your shaft.

Getting the right feel

Getting the length of a stick right for a player's physique is a vital aid to dribbling the puck or ball with maximum efficiency. The correct length is determined by standing in your skates and placing the stick vertically upright, with the tip of the blade on the floor. As a general rule, the butt end (top) should be between your sternum (breast-bone) and your chin. Cut the stick carefully to the right length using a hacksaw. If the toe (outer) end of the blade is off the floor when you are standing in the hocker player's basic stance, the stick is too long or the 'lie' of the blade too high.

Juniors should not be tempted to select Senior sticks and cut them down to fit. Senior shafts are thicker and the blades longer, making it difficult for a smaller player to maintain proper control of them.

The flexibility of the stick should be proportional to the strength and weight of a player, and younger, lighter players tend to need a more flexible shaft than older, heavier players. You can test the flex by holding the stick in the basic stance and pressing down on it.

A curve in a blade can improve the speed or precision of certain forehand shots, but do not attempt to change the shape of the blade by applying heat which will severely weaken the blade and shorten its life. As you gain experience you will develop your own preference for the curve and shape of a blade, and should be able to satisfy your requirements from the wide range of styles available commercially.

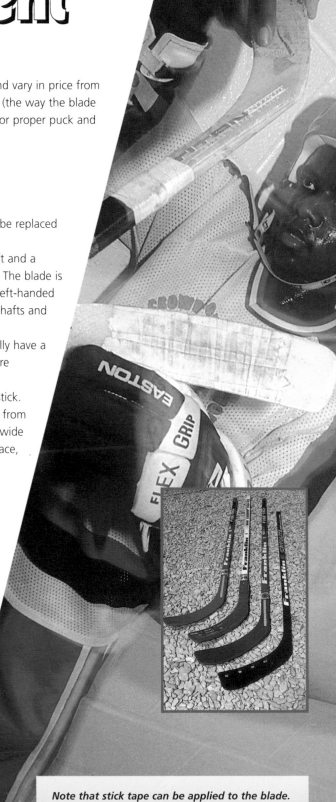

Note that stick tape can be applied to the blade. This will help prolong its life and will also help to cushion the impact of the puck or ball, and so give you better control. When applying tape, always start from the heel of the blade and work towards the toe.

CHOOSING SKATES

Skates are a very important part of a hockey player's equipment, and are generally specifically designed for the job. Proper hockey skates have laces only, and do not use clips which may come undone or get broken due to impact during play. Top-quality boot construction is generally stitched, with one-piece plastic moulded boots available in the lower price ranges.

Favoured wheel sizes are between 72mm and 78mm diameter with a durometer between 74A and 84A depending on the surface being used for the game. The larger the wheels, the more power you can generate, and the more efficient your stride.

Correctly fitting boots should have firm, tightened laces, but these should not be pulled so tight that circulation of the foot is impaired. The toes should feather the toecap, and not be curled or cramped in any way. Room for growth must be allowed for younger players, but care should be taken not to leave too much room. A good skate stockist that specializes in hockey will advise on proper fitting and after-care for your skates. Always buy the best you can afford, but remember that an expensive pair of skates will not improve bad technique – that can only be done with practice. It is much more important that you simply feel comfortable in them.

◁ *Typical top class hockey skates feature stitched construction and lace up fastening.*

The right fit

When buying skates, remember that they are constructed to meet the foot's requirements. Badly fitting skates can result in premature break-down of the boot, regardless of its quality. Fitting gauges only indicate approximate size, and should not be considered a true fit which can only be properly obtained by trying skates on and skating around in them.

A stitched boot should fit basically the same as your regular shoe size does, while a one-piece moulded boot may fit as much as 1 to 1.5 sizes up. To make things even more complicated, you have to remember that many top hockey boots are American, and shoe sizes differ slightly from the UK, with an American 10 being equivalent to a UK 9 and so on.

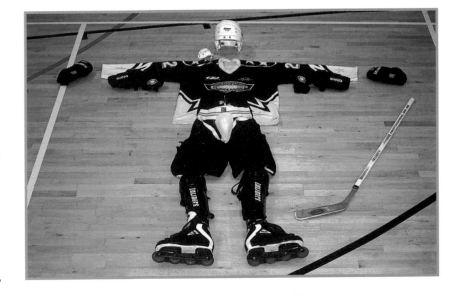

△ *Playing hockey as a 'contact sport' requires the right gear to play safely.*

HELMETS & FACE GUARDS

Helmets and face guards are essential safety equipment for hockey players. All hockey helmets are adjustable, and are equipped with mounting holes to receive face guards. They must fit snugly without being too tight, and must meet the required safety standards.

Putting it on

To get the correct measurement for a helmet, place a tape measure one inch (2.54cm) above the eyebrows and measure the distance (circumference) around the head. Position the helmet on the head so the rim is one finger-width above the eyebrows, and gradually begin to downsize the helmet until a comfortable fit is achieved. Tighten and secure the adjusting screws, and adjust the chin strap to its proper fitting. The helmet must be snug enough to prevent rotation or slip. Be very careful, as wearing an oversize helmet could cause injuries.

Full-face or half-visors?

Face guards are either full-face mesh guards or clear guards which are full-face or half-visors. There is also a type of guard available which is half cage and half visor.

To get the correct fit for a full-face guard, position the helmet one finger-width above the eyebrows and then measure the linear distance between the brim and the bottom of the chin. The chin cup of the guard should fit comfortably on the chin with the mouth closed. Be careful here! A guard which is too long can impact on the mouth or nose during play, and that can cause an unpleasant and unnecessary injury.

Half-visors are normally worn by senior players and referees. These should be fitted so there is sufficient clearance between the visor, eyes and nose. Note that hockey face guards must be approved for use with specific helmets – your local supplier will provide all the advice and necessary assistance to help you make the right choice to play safely.

General protection
With all equipment, determine the level of play that you will be involved in and buy equipment suitable for that level. When you are dressed ready to play, you should feel comfortable and not cramped in any way. The only way to get correctly fitting equipment is to try it on, preferably in conjunction with any existing equipment which you are using. Do not be too shy to take your own equipment along to your supplier – it is vital to make sure any new purchases fit correctly.

△ *Make sure the helmet fits perfectly. This is Jay Cardiner, Captain of the Pacer Leisure Enforcers looking happy with his choice.*

◁ *The goalie is there to be shot at, and needs to dress accordingly. As well as blocking most of the goal, all that gear will prevent injury from a very fast-moving puck or ball.*

GLOVES & PADS

Gloves come in sizes ranging from nine to 15 inches (23 to 38cm). To determine the correct size, measure the distance between the tips of your fingers and the crease at the elbow with your forearm bent. The palm of the glove should be reasonably pliable, and the thumb must offer good protection. Padding should be dense to avoid damage to your hand from opponents' sticks.

Gloves must fit properly. This means not being so large that you cannot 'feel' the stick, nor so small that your finger tips are jammed up against the ends.

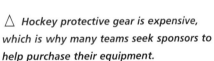

△ *Hockey protective gear is expensive, which is why many teams seek sponsors to help purchase their equipment.*

Elbow pads

When elbow pads are fastened securely, there should be no gap between the pad and either the biceps extension of the shoulder pad or the cuff of the glove. Players who wear a short-cuff-style glove should choose a longer model elbow pad to compensate for loss of protection.

To measure for elbow pads, take the length between the shoulder pad, biceps pad and cuff of the glove. Do not select pads that slip around when secured. These are too big, and may cause – rather than prevent – injury.

Shoulder pads (Body armour)

Shoulder pads should fit snugly, while the vital tips of the shoulder must be positioned under the shoulder cups. The bicep pads should not interfere with the player's elbow pads. The rib and chest protector should not be too long, as this will cause hockey shorts to push the shoulder pads up and so inhibit the player in playing and skating.

To fit shoulder pads, take the player's chest measurement just below the armpits. There are special shoulder pads made with pre-formed chest protectors, to fit ladies.

Shorts & girdles

Girdles are snug-fitting, and are worn under short or long coveralls. Shorts fit less snugly, and are usually worn without coveralls. Shorts should reach the top of the knee and extend to cover the kidneys and lower ribs. The hip, kidney and tailbone pads should cover all critical areas.

Girdles should fit very snugly so the padding stays in place, covering all critical areas. They should not be so tight as to restrict movement. The girdle should extend from the top of the knee to cover the kidneys and lower rib cage.

Shin guards

Shin guards are made in a variety of lengths from nine to 16 inches (23 to 41cm). Sizes are measured from the centre of the knee to the top of the skate. Shin guards which are too long will ride up so that the knee cup is above the knee, offering little protection.

Do not hold shin guards in place with very tight socks. Use heavy elastic shin-guard straps or leg tape to hold the guards securely in place.

EQUIPMENT TIPS

◆ The butt end of a hockey stick can be highly dangerous if it is fallen on, poked through a face-cage or up under a visor. In many games it is mandatory to fit a protective butt-end to reduce the threat of injury, a precaution which makes even more sense with aluminium and composite handles. You can make your own butt-end protector using standard thick tape, building up a pad at the top and then continuing to tape down the handle to improve the stick's non-slip qualities around the grip.

◆ Do not paint your helmet. Many paint solvents attack plastics, melting them or making them brittle.

◆ Perspex visors tend to mist up. Cure this by using a demist solution designed for motorcyclists' visors. Alternatively, wipe a tiny amount of washing-up liquid or shower gel onto the visor for the same result.

◆ Never wash hockey gloves, however bad they smell! It will dry out the leather, making them inflexible and prone to splitting. The best way to get rid of any smell is to hang out your gloves to air. Do not use deodorants either, which may also damage the leather.

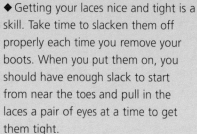

◆ Getting your laces nice and tight is a skill. Take time to slacken them off properly each time you remove your boots. When you put them on, you should have enough slack to start from near the toes and pull in the laces a pair of eyes at a time to get them tight.

◆ Work your way up each boot to make the laces tight all the way, but not too tight over the bridge of your foot which can cut off the blood supply and cause numbing. To finish, the laces need to be pulled tightest at the top four pairs of eyes which will give firm ankle support.

◆ Avoid 'lace pullers' which direct all the force on one point on each lace and soon break them.

WHEELS AND BEARINGS

No matter how good a skater you are, you will not succeed if you don't have enough grip from your wheels to transfer all that power into speed and maintain control. There are huge numbers of wheels to choose from, and no one set is going to be perfect for everyone. A number of factors will determine what type of wheel you should use:

1. Weight

If you are light, you do not exert the same amount of pressure on your wheels which will give you less grip. Consequently you need a softer wheel.

Some wheels do not work as designed with lightweight players, for instance air-cushioned wheels do not compress so well when worn by players under eight stone (51kg). Even though they are soft and have good grip, they will not compress properly to give a cushioned ride as designed.

2. Style

The way you skate will also depend on the hardness or 'durometer rating' of the wheel – the higher the number, the harder the wheel compound. The stopping technique that you use will define your choice of wheel, and also your cornering. You will find that factor, in conjunction with your weight and the floor will determine whether you need harder or softer wheels.

3. Floor surface

The surface on which you skate makes a big difference to the sort of wheel you should use. Different surfaces have different durometer ratings as do wheels, so softer floors will give you more grip.

◆ Polished concrete is the hardest floor. If it has not been sealed with a resin finish, it can be very slippery, so very soft wheels are a must.

◆ Groundwood floors are made from wood and synthetic particles compressed in a resin. It is probably the most popular form of floor in modern sports halls as they are durable and hard-wearing, but are not as hard as concrete. A slightly harder wheel will work here.

◆ Sprung wooden floors are nice to skate on as they have a reverse suspension effect and 'give'. It is not as fast a surface to skate on, as some of the power that is laid down with the boot is absorbed by the sprung floor.

◁ *Dressing up for the game ahead is a slow and careful process.*

4. Rockering skates

On a lot of skates it is possible to raise the front and back wheels, which is to 'rocker' them. This leaves only the two centre wheels in contact with the ground when the skate is flat, and it allows the skate to make tighter turns and be more manoeuvrable as it emulates the ice skate (most ice blades have a rockered profile). There is a drawback to this. You lose traction, and as a result your speed and stopping performance is degraded.

Some skates allow you to rocker your wheels by having reversible plastic inserts in the chassis, but many manufacturers exclude these from their metal chassis and the cheapest of skates do not have the facility either. There is a way round this: use different diameter wheels. Normally you should use the largest diameter wheel that your skate can take.

Many skaters go further and vary the hardness of their wheels, some preferring to have harder wheels in the centre (where they wear more since they are in contact with the floor more often than the rockered wheels at either end), and some putting softer wheels in the centre to make up for the lack of grip caused to only having two wheels on the floor at any one time. In the end it is a matter of personal preference.

◁ *So much to plan and think about, not least getting the right wheels for the floor!*

5. Wheel profiles

The profile is the outline or side-cut of the surface of the wheel in contact with the ground. It determines how much of the wheel surface is in contact with the ground. The wider the profile, the more stability and traction (better for goalies) it will give. The narrower the wheel, the faster it goes due to less friction.

What wheels you use depends very much on the condition of wooden floors you skate on. If they are newly varnished a harder wheel will work, but if it is an old floor which is dusty, you should use a softer wheel. It is possible, if you are heavy and the floor is reasonably grippy, that your wheels will judder on the floor as they lose grip and then catch again, leaving minute bits of your wheel behind like a rubber on wooden desk!

◆ Linoleum is probably the softest type of floor you will come across. You can get away with a fairly hard wheel, but when you lose grip, the breakaway is sudden and total. A medium wheel is recommended here as it gives enough grip, but not too much.

◆ Sport Court is the best surface and some day all floors will be made this way! This surface consists of a number of interlocking plastic tiles which are solid for indoors, but they also have a meshed type tile that is also available for outdoors. The indoor tile is the surface chosen by Roller Hockey International (RHI) in the USA.

◆ Tarmac is the mortal enemy of the soft tyre. Anything less than an 84A is going to get shredded in a matter of hours. If you pop out for a bit of pick-up hockey, make sure you change those wheels!

▷ *Puck or Ball? Another choice for hockey players.*

◁ *You can go to town with all types of hockey wheels, but in the end it's the player's skill that makes the difference.*

6. Bearings

The more you pay, the better and faster bearings you will usually get. However, for less experienced hockey players a major investment in high ABEC rating wheels is likely to be a waste of money with ultimate bearing performance only being of relevance to speed skaters.

Hockey Games

In the UK there are a number of organizations which play hockey at amateur level, but confusingly play different games under different rules.

British Skater Hockey Association (BSHA)

The British Skater Hockey Association plays 'skater hockey', mainly playing sports halls and using a pitch similar to that used for 5-a-side football. The game allows ice hockey-style 'body-contact' – giving the possibility of high-speed collisions – but unlike ice hockey it is played with a ball which reveals its pick-up origins.

The BSHA incorporates regional associations with Pee-Wee, Junior and Senior teams, plus a few Women and Minnow teams. It is a member of the International Skater Hockey Association (ISHA) together with Denmark, Germany and Switzerland. The Great Britain Senior Team led by Edutie Edutie and coached by Carl Toppin won the first ISHA Championships held in the autumn of 1997 with the GB Junior Team finishing runners-up to Germany.

△ **Under 10 year olds can play with the Minnows.**

△ *A typical top class Senior team – the Hyper Street Cruisers won the BSHA Shield and National Championships, as well as the Kaarst Cup in the 1996-97 season.*

◁ *The Enforcers Women's Team play other women and Juniors in the LASH (London Area Skater Hockey) League.*

BSHA requirements

The number of players that can be registered as a team squad for any league match or competition.is 16 outfield and two goalkeepers. All players must be registered with the BSHA to play in any league or competition, as must managers, coaches and team/club members who are present on the team bench. The maximum number of players on the court at any one time is five, and unlimited substitutions can be made. Players cannot play for more than one team, but may transfer once during the season for a transfer fee.

Skater hockey is played in four age groups:

◆	Minnows	Up to 10 years old.
◆	Pee Wees	Over 10 but under 14.
◆	Juniors	Over 14 but under 18.
◆	Seniors	Over 18.

The qualifying date for all age groups is taken from 1st September of the season. Mixed skater hockey, with players of both sexes participating, is allowed. Younger players may play in a higher age group with consent from a parent or guardian and permission from the proper authority. Every player in a team must wear the same colour shirt of an approved style, plus an identifying number on the back and arms.

Even though skater hockey is a body-contact sport, injury is rare. However the BSHA stipulates that every player must wear basic protective equipment, and strongly recommends additional equipment if players can afford it. Minimum requirements include a helmet (with chin-strap fastener), elbow pads and knee/shin pads for every match and when training, plus padded shorts and box. Players under 19 must wear a half or full-face visor/cage attached to helmet. Recommended extras include padded gloves, abdominal pads, and shoulder protection. In addition to the minimum requirements, all goalkeepers must wear full mask/visor, padded gloves, shoulder, chest and abdominal pads, padded shorts and goalkeeper's leg pads. Where possible, padded equipment must be worn under team shirts and socks.

Standard ice hockey or street hockey sticks are used in right- or left-handed versions, with different blade angles to suit. The BSHA plays with a ball made of special non-bouncing plastic with a diameter of 60-75mm and maximum weight of 120 grams. The ball may be any colour that can be seen on the pitch. The goal cage must be made of wood or metal strong enough to withstand impact from players, but should not be fixed to the ground. The inside measurement of the goal mouth is 1.85m wide x 1.20m high. Small mesh netting should surround the cage, with a suspended drop net to trap the ball when a goal is scored. A 40m x 20m pitch is desirable for official matches and tournaments. 30m x 15m may be acceptable for training and other matches.

For all matches there must be two qualified referees on pitch, plus an off-pitch timekeeper and scorer who also acts as penalty steward, recording who is sent off and when they may return.

British Inline Puck Hockey Association (BIPHA)

The BIPHA game is played with a puck, and is non-contact. It was formed in response to a demand for hockey on skates, played along similar lines to ice hockey with the speed and accuracy of a puck, but without physical contact which makes it a safer, less stressful game to contest. The game is mainly played in sports halls in the UK, but is ideally experienced on a large rink between 20-30 metres wide and 40-60 metres long. The ideal size has a 1:2 ratio and is approximately the size of an ice hockey rink.

BIPHA is recognized by Federation Internationale de Roller Skating (FIRS) through the National Roller Hockey Association (NRHA), and the FIRS World Championship is held each year, and reflects a big international following for the game. Recent World Championships have been held in the USA (Chicago), Italy and Austria, with the USA winning the 1997 event against teams from Canada, Austria, the Czech Republic, Spain, France, Italy, Switzerland, Argentina, Brazil, Australia, Ecuador, Mexico, Belgium and Great Britain.

BIPHA requirements

The BIPHA game is played predominantly on inline skates, though quads are acceptable for domestic games. The maximum team size is 12 outfield players with two netminders; the minimum team required to start a game is four outfield players and one netminder. All age groups and both sexes are encouraged to play, and there are plans to expand the inital league structure for Seniors (18+), Juniors (14-18) and Juniors U14 to include Under-10s and Women who do not want to play with the men. Senior teams play three periods of 20 minutes, and each team is allowed one time out per period. Other age groups play three periods of 15 minutes, also with one time out per period.

Safety equipment is considered of great importance. No players are allowed to play unless adequately protected. Minimum kit comprises an HECC approved ice hockey-style helmet with full-face cage for all players under 18, ice hockey leg guards and shin guards, gloves and protective cup. Padded shorts and elbow pads are a recommended option.

▷ *Hockey is a dynamic and thrilling sport, with the main UK season starting each autumn and carrying on through the following year.*

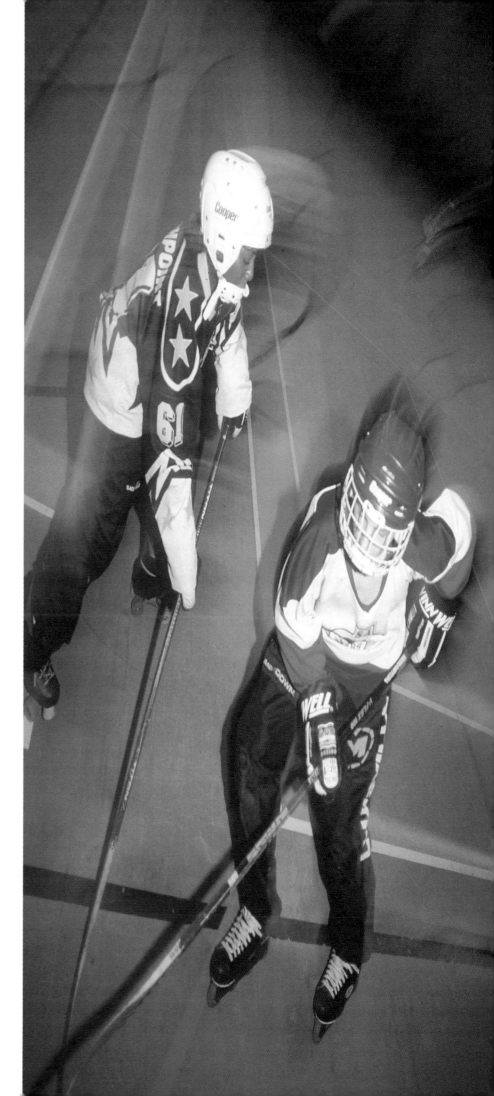

British Rink Hockey Association (BRHA)

BRHA games are similar to BIPHA games in that they are played in sports halls with a puck. However, the BRHA game is closely modelled on ice hockey and allows full body contact. As such it comes nearest to the Roller Hockey International (RHI) Professional League which originated in the USA and Canada and is based on professional ice hockey. Major League Roller Hockey is the other big professional series, also based in the USA and Canada.

The BRHA started with just five teams in 1983, and is affiliated to the British Ice Hockey Association, taking advantage of their internationally recognized insurance and coaching schemes. It organizes the Off Beat Cup challenge tournament. This annual event gives BRHA teams a chance to play against guest teams from the other disciplines, and is the largest hockey tournament held in Britain which is open to all age groups.

BRHA requirements

The BRHA plays in four age groups:

- ◆ Cubs   12 years and under.
- ◆ Colts   14 and under.
- ◆ Juniors   18 and under.
- ◆ Seniors   18 and over with no upper age limit.

All age groups play full body contact. This means all players must wear full ice hockey-spec equipment, with under 16s required to wear full-face cages. Teams play four-on-four plus goalie, with two referees and no linesman. Quad skates are allowed along with inlines.

△ **Debbie Wiles minds the goal for the Warrior Women.**

▷ **The referee plays a vital role in hockey. Many refs opt to wear inlines so they can keep up with the game!**

△ **The Enforcer Women get ready to take on the S. A. Junior Bears.**

Hockey Techniques

BASIC STANCE

The Ready Position: The basic stance allows a player to move in any direction – forwards, backwards or sideways from a solid, well-balanced base of support.

◆ The feet are shoulder-width apart with the toes pointing slightly outwards.

◆ Knees and ankles are slightly bent at an angle of approximately 45 degrees.

◆ The upper body leans slightly forward, with the weight on the balls of the feet.

◆ The shoulders, knees and toes are directly over each other, so they could be joined by an imaginary perpendicular straight line.

◆ The head is up with the eyes looking forward.

◆ The stick is held with both hands, one hand at the butt end of the shaft with the other hand approx. 12 to 15 inches (30 to 38cm) below. The fingers and thumb are wrapped around the shaft, with the thumb and first finger of each hand forming two V's on the top side of the shaft. The blade is flat on the floor in front, and slightly to the side of the body.

POWER SKATING

The skating stride can be broken down into four basic steps. Whether skating forwards, backwards, doing crossovers or starting, all the elements of your stride can be compared to the motions of a tennis racket. Both require a three-part process – a wind-up, a release, and a follow-through. The skating stride requires one additional element – the return.

▷ *Playing hockey is the surest way to master a range of inline techniques as quickly as possible.*

▷ *Power skating up to a position where you are ready to take a shot on goal.*

1. Wind-up

The wind-up is like the backward swing of the racket. This acts to 'coil a spring'. The more you coil it up, the more force it will have when you release it. For the wind-up you must utilize the inside edge of the skate that is going to be applying the thrust. It must grip the floor. Without the wheels gripping and without your body weight pressing down over the thrusting edge, you have no way to get traction. When you try to thrust without traction, your wheels will slide rather than grip the floor.

The more inside edge you use to grip the floor, and the more you press your weight down over the edge, the more resistance you will have to provide a strong thrust. Press into the floor with your edge, knee and body weight. This downward pressure continues the wind-up, and determines how effective your thrust will be.

SKATING ON EDGES

Each skate has two edges – the inside and outside edges. Although both edges play a role in propulsion, the inside edge is primarily used for thrusting or driving. The outside edge is sometimes used for propulsion, but is primarily for turning. Good skaters use all four edges. Look at your wheels. If you have wear only on the inside edges, this indicates that your stance is too wide. Try to adopt a more upright position with the gliding leg under your body. Speed is not important at the beginning. Good technique, coupled with the correct application of power, will eventually give you the speed you need to compete at any level.

2. Release

The release is the actual leg thrust, and can be compared to the swinging of the racket. The more effective your leg thrusts, the more power you will get. You must utilize your leg muscles, strongly and properly. Many hockey players are unaware of how strongly their legs must work to get maximum power.

To achieve a good release, thrust your leg powerfully out against the edge which is gripping the floor. With each push your legs should feel the strain of the work you are doing. If your legs don't feel the strain, they are not working thoroughly.

3. Follow-through

Thrusting without a full follow-through is like swinging a racket and then stopping your swing as you contact the ball. The result in both cases is a great loss of power and drive.

At the very end of each thrust, the thrusting leg must be fully extended away from your body so it is completely straight with the knee locked. Only after reaching this position has the leg finished its pushing. Many players, in an attempt to move their legs quickly when they skate, never give their legs that little extra time which is needed to reach full extension, and therefore never realize their full power.

▷ *Jay Gardiner skates with the ball while training with the Enforcers.*

4. The return

After reaching full extension, the thrusting leg must now return under your body. Your weight is transferred and you prepare for the other leg to thrust in turn.

The return is a very important and often neglected part of the stride. If the leg does not return so that both feet are directly under your body, you cannot get a good wind-up for the next thrusting skate. Every push must start with your feet centred underneath you. The 'wide stance' which hockey players supposedly use is a myth, and should only be used for stability when gliding on two feet. In order to achieve a powerful thrust, always begin a stride with your feet well centred under your body.

FORWARD CROSSOVERS

Forward crossovers are all about increasing your mobility. They are used to change direction while attempting to gain speed.

Ready to go

All skating movements begin with the basic stance or 'ready' position. The key points are always the same:

◆ Feet are placed shoulder-width apart with your toes pointing slightly inwards.
◆ Knees and ankles are flexed at approximately 45 degrees.
◆ Your upper body leans slightly forward, with your shoulders over your knees and your knees over your toes.
◆ Keep your head up.
◆ Hold the stick in both hands, with the blade flat on the floor and slightly to the side of your body.

Start moving

Begin forward skating as normal. Make sure you are transferring your weight to your gliding skate. Then, when you are nice and comfortable with your skating action, begin your crossovers. Right-handed players find it easiest to cross over with their right foot – i.e. the right foot crosses over the left foot. We will assume a right-handed player in this description.

Do not travel too fast at first, and allow a large turning circle. Turn your head and shoulders to the left, as this is the direction you will take. When your shoulders have turned, your body will begin to move in that direction. Keep your gliding foot (the left foot) steady, and lift your back foot (right foot) over and across your gliding foot. Transfer your weight to your right foot, and repeat the same operation for as many times as you need to complete the turn. Once the turn is finished, return to normal skating. Take a few more forward strides, and then continue with some more crossovers.

Getting it right

When you are doing your crossovers, keep your upper body still, two hands on your stick with the blade on the floor. Then, when you have mastered forward right crossovers, move on and try to master forward left crossovers. Remember that speed is not important at this stage. It's proper technique that provides the basis for future speed.

Russian circles

One of the best exercises for practising crossovers is Russian circles. Use the three circles on a basketball court, or lay out three circles using small cones or

An experienced hockey player can skate where he wants and when he wants, without ever seeming to look at the puck or ball. You always try to skate 'head-up' in hockey.

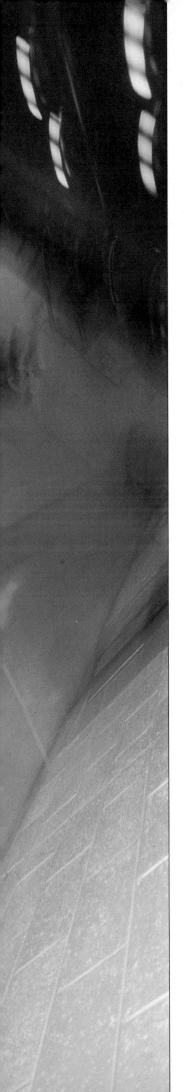

markers. This will give you plenty of practice on crossovers on both feet. Remember to keep your stick on the floor with the blade held in the circle, ready to take an imaginary pass. Also, keep your head up.

1. Skate one circle clockwise, crossing right over left.
2. Skate forwards to the second circle.
3. Skate anti-clockwise round the second circle, crossing left over right .
4. Skate forwards to the third circle.
5. Skate clockwise round the third circle, crossing right over left.
6. Skate forwards and turn back to the circles.
7. Skate round circles one and three anti-clockwise and circle two clockwise.

Perfect crossovers

When you have gained some confidence in crossovers, you are ready to perfect your technique. Do not lift your back foot too high, and practise keeping your wheels on the floor whilst sliding your crossover foot in front of and across the gliding foot. The gliding foot then becomes the back foot. As you begin to transfer your weight to your front foot, you drive the outside edge of the wheels of your back skate hard into the floor to give forward propulsion.

The ability to master crossovers so you can change direction and execute tight turns is a must for all hockey players in a sport where stopping is likely to be neither easy nor efficient. They may seem difficult to master at first, but with a little practice forward crossovers become easy.

BACKWARD SKATING

Backward skating is an essential skill to master if you are to become an effective hockey player.

Starting off

Stand in the basic 'ready' stance, but take your bottom hand off the stick with your elbow flexed. Point your toes slightly inwards. Bend your knees and sit back in the stance, keeping your back straight and your head up. Place the blade of the stick flat on the floor in front of you, with the toe of the blade pointing in. Now you are ready to go.

Try C-Cuts

The basic backwards skating technique is known as 'C-Cuts'. This is the preferred method which maximizes speed and efficiency whilst retaining balance. The technique utilizes only one foot at a time, with the other foot being used as balance.

△ *In hockey you need to be ready to skate backwards at any time...*

Allow your right skate to lean onto the inside edge, and then push away from your body before bringing it back underneath yourself. You will notice that this motion creates a 'C' on the floor. It is important that the foot which is not engaged in the 'C-Cut' is kept still under the body.

Remember the key points in order to get it right:
◆ Assume the basic 'ready' stance and adjust for backwards skating with your bottom hand off the stick as described above.
◆ Rotate the heel of the driving leg outwards, press down on your inside edge, and extend your hip, knee and ankle forwards and sideways to describe a 'C'-shaped arc on the floor.
◆ Transfer the full weight of your body to the gliding skate during the thrust, ensuring that you are comfortable and well-balanced on this skate.
◆ Return your thrusting skate under your body, then initiate a fresh backward thrust with your other skate.

Remember

1. Resist the urge to lean forwards too far while moving backwards. This will result in loss of balance as your weight is transferred onto your toes and away from the ball of the foot where it belongs.
2. Flex the knee of the gliding leg to allow a long thrust by the thrusting leg.
3. Keep your bottom still, and avoid transferring body weight by swinging your hips.

Forward Crossovers

Jay Gardiner follows the
ball around the court with
a perfect succession of
forward crossovers.

Forward Crossovers

Backward Crossovers

Jay Gardiner also shows that backward crossovers can come in handy.

BACKWARD CROSSOVERS
How to do them
1. From a basic backward stance position, turn the hips and trunk slightly towards the direction of the crossover. Keep your head up, facing the oncoming opponent.
2. Extend the inside leg forward, and press the outside edge of the skate hard into the floor.
3. Keeping your stride short with your skate close to the floor, cross the outside leg over and in front of the inside leg as it extends.
4. Bring the outside skate down on the floor, and press hard on the inside edge.

Why use it?
Other than for a rapid backward start, backward crossovers are not very effective in hockey. The opposing player can very easily catch you on the wrong foot, and will have two or three paces start on you. It would be more effective to master forward or backward pivots off either foot.

Practice makes perfect
Practice slowly at first, allowing yourself plenty of space. Remember to keep two hands on your stick, and avoid flailing the stick about. When you have completed the pivot, remove your bottom hand from your stick. To pivot faster, bring the skates close together and straighten the body just before pivoting. This will lengthen the vertical axis and increase the speed of rotation. Bringing the arms closer to the body also helps increase rotation speed.

FORWARD TO BACKWARD PIVOTS
A forward to backward pivot allows the player to change from moving forwards to backwards without modifying speed. Forward to backward pivots are essential to defend forward rushes by attacking players effectively.

How to do them
1. The pivot is initiated from the regular skating stride. Transfer the weight of the body over the gliding leg, opposite to the intended pivot side. For example, if you want to turn to the right, transfer the weight to the left skate. Hold your stick in both hands.
2. At the end of your stride (gliding on your left skate), straighten up and rotate your right skate (back foot) outwards through 180 degrees, bringing it to the other side of the gliding skate (right foot) facing in the opposite direction.
3. Then rotate your head and shoulders to the right, and transfer your weight at the same time to the right skate. Rotate the left skate through 180 degrees to bring it parallel to the right skate.
4. As the pivot ends, the blade of the stick should be immediately put down on the floor in front of the player and the bottom hand removed from the stick.

Stick Handling

S tick handling and associated puck or ball control are an important part of hockey, closely related to dribbling a football – and mastery of them often elevates good players to great players. Good execution of stick-handling skills can be aided by chosing the correct length of stick and gloves which suit you.

How to master it

All skating and stick-handling movements begin with the basic stance or 'ready' position. Once again, the key points are:

- Feet shoulder-width apart, with the toes pointing slightly outwards.
- Knees and ankles flexed at approximately 45 degrees.
- Upper body leaning slightly forwards, with the shoulders over the knees and knees over the toes.
- Head up.
- Stick held in both hands, with the blade flat on the floor and slightly to the side of the body.

Stick handling is a precise skill which allows the player to skate with the puck or ball.

Assume the basic stance and check that your hands are in the correct position. Your top hand should hold the butt (top) end of the stick, with your lower hand approximately 12in (30cm) down the shaft. Your thumbs and first fingers should form parallel V's on the shaft.

Cup the puck or ball in the curve of the blade while facing forwards, look down at it, and then slowly raise your head until you are looking forwards while keeping the puck or ball in your field of peripheral vision at the same time. All players at first have a tendency to look down at the puck or ball, but it is essential to be able to keep your head up to see the play developing around you. Standing still in the ready position, start to move the puck or ball at about shoulder width from side to side. Ensure you roll your wrists so you do not lose control of it. Do not grip the shaft too tightly. Your grip should allow you to feel the puck or ball, while retaining full control of the stick. Cup the puck or ball in the centre of the blade, cushioning it while you are stick handling.

Slide the blade of the stick along the floor. Do not bang it on the floor! There should be very little noise created by the stick. Move the puck or ball on your forehand, lift the blade over it, and move it on your backhand in the opposite direction. Avoid exaggerated movements. The blade must stay very close to the puck or ball or be in contact with it to ensure proper control. While stick handling, your arms should be held away from your body for ease of movement with a fluid, comfortable style.

STICK-HANDLING TECHNIQUES

Side-to-side stick handling: Move the puck or ball in front of you from side-to-side, forehand to backhand. Be sure to keep your weight over the top of the puck or ball and do not move it too wide. You must always be comfortably in control.

Back-to-front stick handling: This is the same as side-to-side stick handling, but the puck or ball is moved off to one side of the body, forehand to backhand.

Backward stick handling: Stick handling while skating backwards requires the puck or ball to be drawn towards the body in a side-to-side motion. This is an essential skill for defence men.

Do not overuse stick handling. It is an essential skill when manoeuvring at close quarters, but on a breakaway, stick handling will slow you down, so just push the ball in front of you.

STICK-HANDLING DRILLS

'Drills' are used to practise hockey skills. First practise the drills without a puck or ball to get used to the quick transitions. Keep your stick down on the floor, and keep your head up to develop team awareness while your peripheral vision keeps track of the puck or ball. With all drills start slowly and build up speed gradually as your skills develop. When you have finished, repeat all drills in the opposite direction to give practice on all four edges of your blades, as well as exercising both forehand and backhand.

Drill No 1

Assume the ready position. Stand still and practise side-to-side and back-to-front stick handling, swapping from one to the other after each series of ten movements. Keep your head up, and get accustomed to using your peripheral vision. Pretend that you are in a game, looking round for a team mate to receive your pass.

Drill No 2

Place six cones on the floor in two parallel lines of three set approximately ten feet (3m) apart. Skating forwards, carry the puck or ball using side-to-side movements. The stick leads around each cone first, with the skater following.

Drill No 3

Using the same six cones as Drill No 2, repeat the drill but make a 360 degree turn on Cones 1 and 6. The turn on Cone 1 should be anti-clockwise and on Cone 6 clockwise. Cup the puck or ball in the centre of the blade when making tight turns.

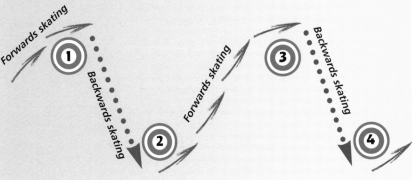

△ *Stick handling skills lead on to passing and making shots on goal.*

Drill No 4

This incorporates forwards and backwards stick handling. When you skate backwards, the puck or ball must be cupped in the centre of the blade and drawn towards your body.

Place four cones on the floor as shown below. Skate forwards to Cone 1. As soon as your skates pass the cone, change to backwards skating and carry the puck or ball on to Cone 2. As soon as your skates pass Cone 2, change to forwards skating. Repeat the drill on Cones 3 and 4.

Forwards skating ① Backwards skating ② Forwards skating ③ Backwards skating ④

PASSING

Passing the puck or ball to a teammate can be performed both forehand and backhand. The player who makes the pass must take account of his team mate's speed and relative position, in order to direct the pass to where it can be intercepted.

Receiving a pass

Most problems occur when a player receives a pass and the puck or ball either bounces up and over the blade or rebounds off it at an angle. It is all a matter of controlling the hit, which is done by angling the blade to hold the puck or ball down and letting it give a little on receipt of the pass so there is no rebound. You can practise your own pass drills by skating alongside a wall, and using it to bounce back passes which you can take on the forehand and backhand.

◆ Adjust your speed and position to line up for the pass.
◆ Make sure you are holding the stick properly, one hand firmly at the top butt end and the other with a good grip up to two feet (60cm) down the shaft.
◆ Hold the stick so that the blade is square-on to the oncoming puck or balll. Angle the blade down onto the floor, so it forms a wedge into which the puck or ball will slide without bouncing over the top.
◆ As the puck or ball hits, let the stick give a little with your lower arm so its impact is cushioned.

Backhand pass

Taking a pass is more difficult on the backhand than on the forehand, since the blade is working against you with the puck or ball hitting a convex curve. The technique is basically the same.

◆ Turn to face the puck or ball square-on.
◆ Move the stick across your body to create a wedge angle which the puck or ball cannot bounce over.
◆ Cushion the pass by easing back on the stick.

▷ *Time to pass the puck or ball to a team mate who can make a clear shot on goal.*

▽ *A player moves to intercept a pass and take control.*

SHOOTING

◆ The wrist shot is accomplished by a quick flick of the wrists with a correspondingly short forwards movement of the blade. It is a highly accurate shot, but nothing like as powerful as the slap shot.

◆ The slap shot requires a full movement of the stick, bringing the blade back, lifting it high, and swinging it down hard. The blade is directed to hit the ground just behind the puck or ball, bending the stick and flicking the blade into the puck or ball to drive it forwards with maximum power.

◆ The snap shot is halfway between the wrist shot and slap shot, with the stick swung back to a horizontal position. It is fast and accurate up to 33 feet (10m) out from the goal.

△ *The goal tender is ready and waiting to intercept high speed shots at all times.*

Slap-shot skills

1. Put your weight on your back leg with your knees slightly bent.
2. Hands should be about two feet (60cm) apart on the stick, with the bottom hand lower than usual.
3. Keep your head up and look at the target, letting your peripheral vision keep track of the puck or ball.
4. Swing your stick right back until the back arm is horizontal with the blade lifted past 45 degrees to the ground. (The stick is only lifted to a horizontal position for a snap shot.)
5. Bring the stick down fast, moving your weight onto your front leg.
6. The blade is aimed to 'slap' the ground less than one inch (2.5cm) behind the puck or ball, creating a whiplash effect which accelerates the blade forwards.
7. Follow the shot through, bringing your butt hand in close to your body and letting your bottom hand swing with the stick until it is pointing forwards horizontally.

Snap-shot skills

1. Keep your hands in the normal stick-handling position, with the puck or ball held in the centre of the blade.
2. Flick your wrists back from the target.
3. Snap your lower hand forwards, while pulling your butt hand back to fire the shot.
4. Follow through with the swing, shifting your weight forward and looking for a possible rebound off the goal.

◁ *A snap shot flicks the puck or ball towards the goal.*

Skate Maintenance

Skates require a certain amount of maintenance if they are put to hard use, though compared to running something like a mountain bike, the costs and amount of time required are relatively low.

Equipment

Most skates have a standard 4mm Allen key fitting for removing the wheels and cuff. It is worth investing in a special skate tool such as the 3-way Gripz which combines 4mm and $^1/_8$ in Hex keys (Allen keys) with a Phillips head screwdriver and two 'bearing pushers'. The bearing pushers are used to get the bearing cassettes out of the wheels.

Work area

Prepare your own personal space on which to work, which can be left without interference and will stay clean. The cleaner your work area, the more organized and confident your regular maintenance will be. Lay down sheets of paper which can be thrown away when dirty, and secure them if necessary. The paper should be a light colour and reasonably resistant to crud and liquid, so that you can keep track of all the bits coming out of your skates without losing them in the grime.

Work practice

It is vital to keep all the bits in order, taking them out one at a time, laying them down, and noting the sequence for re-assembly.
1. Take all bolts out.
2. Take all wheels out with any spacers or washers.
3. Push out the two bearings cassettes from each wheel.
4. Open up each bearing cassette (if serviceable).
5. Clean and lubricate each bearing cassette and put them back in the wheels.
6. Clean up the chassis and outer boots. Check for damage to the buckles or inner boots, and replace laces if necessary.
7. Put the wheels back in the chassis, and tighten the bolts.

Cleaning bearings

Bearings are the bits with which most people have maintenance problems. It is worth taking time to keep them working perfectly – only then can you

1. Lay out all your equipment cleanly and neatly.

3. Get all the crud and carbage off the wheels and examine them for wear.

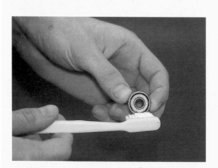

5. Use a tooth brush to clean all the dust and dirt off the bearings.

7. Take great care with all those little balls!

2. Take out the wheels and clean up the chassis. What a mess!

4. Remove the bearings using a bearing pusher.

6. Use some kind of pin to remove the c-clip and reveal the inner workings.

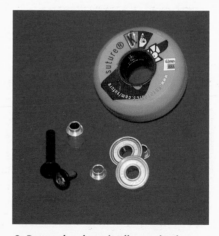

8. Remember how it all goes back together? Stay tidy and you'll be OK.

enjoy your skating to the maximum. Bearing cassettes can be non-serviceable (NS) or fully serviceable (FS).

NS: To look after the bearings in a non-serviceable cassette, make a regular practice of cleaning all the dust and grime from the outer surfaces with a toothbrush and dry cloth. To do this, remove them from the wheels as necessary. If the bearings start to grind and run badly, all you can safely do is replace the cassette with a new one.

FS: A fully serviceable bearing cassette can be stripped down, cleaned, lubricated and reassembled. Use a pin or safety pin to prise out the 'C-ring' which runs round the inner circumference of the shield and holds it in place. You can then use the point to push out the shield, and get access to the bearings.

It is vital to use a non-corrosive, citrus-based bearing cleaner which is specially designed for use with inliners and will not rust your bearings. Soak the exposed bearings in the cleaner for a short time, wearing rubber gloves to protect your skin. After five minutes the dirt will start to flow off, and you can then use a soft bristle toothbrush or cloth to wipe out any remaining grime.

When you are satisfied that the bearings are clean enough, remove them from the liquid and gently shake or blow on them until they are fairly dry, being sure to avoid all contact with your eyes and lips. Wait until the remnants of citrus cleaner have evaporated before applying any lubricant.

As with the cleaner, you should use a lubricant specifically designed for inline bearings – some bearing sets are sold complete with a small lubricant bottle. Gently squeeze a drop of lubricant onto each ball, clean and replace the shield, and lock it with the C-ring. Finally put a thin layer of lubricant round the edge of the outer bearing where the writing is. This will help to keep water and dust out of the bearings.

Reassembling wheels

Before putting the wheels back in, make sure you clean off all the bolts, spacers and rocker washers if you have them. You don't want to ruin all that hard work cleaning and lubricating by transferring grime from the bolts and washers back into the bearings. You should also clean the chassis thoroughly.

Remember, take care of your gear and it will take care of you

SKATE MAINTAIN-SENSE

◆ Never skate in the wet, unless you know you have waterproof bearings.
◆ Avoid skating through mud, gravel or sand which can all do terrible things to your bearings and wheels.
◆ Use serviceable bearings – they last longer.
◆ Make a regular practice of tightening the bolts which hold the wheels. Do not over-tighten them, or you may damage a bearing cassette.
◆ Keep a supply of spare bolts and washers, in case you break or lose them.
◆ It is possible to break the top off a bolt. If this happens, you can saw a slot across the top with a hacksaw and use a screwdriver to unscrew the bolt.
◆ If your inner boot splits, you can normally order a replacement.
◆ Always do up the buckles on skates when you take them off. It's easy to trip over abandoned skates, and open buckles are easily broken.
◆ Clean and service your skates at regular intervals.

Glossary | Useful Addresses

Inline skating has its own language, particularly when it comes to the aggressive scene. This is no more than a selection of some of the words you may come across…

ABEC: Annular Bearing Engineering Council rating for smooth running bearings.

Airs (aggressive): Aerial moves when a skater takes off on a ramp or jumps gaps and stairs.

Allen key: A hexagonal tool for turning bolts – the prime tool for stripping down skates.

Alley Oop (aggressive): A trick done backwards – e.g. Alley-Oop Pornstar.

Anti-rocker (aggressive): Smaller inside wheels than outside wheels – typically 49m inside and 62mm outside – to facilitate grinding between the middle two wheels. The same effect is achieved by rockering the middle wheels upwards.

ASA (aggressive): The Aggressive Skaters' Association runs a professional world tour.

Backhand (hockey): Handling the puck or ball with the back of the blade.

Backside (aggressive): Facing outwards – e.g. on a kerb with your back to the pavement, grinding backside first'.

Barrel Roll: A move which combines skating round in a circle and spinning at the same time.

Bearing pusher: A simple tool which pushes the bearings out of the wheel.

Bio (aggressive): An aerial move, spinning with your body parallel to the ground.

BIPHA (hockey): British Inline Puck Hockey Association.

Body checking (hockey): Body contact when two players collide.

Bone-over (aggressive): Bending one or both ankles over to the limit when grinding topside moves.

Bowl (aggressive): A concrete or wooden bowl sunk into the ground.

BRHA (hockey): British Rink Hockey Association.

BSHA (hockey): British Skater Hockey Association.

Cab (aggressive): A visual side spin (the way you can see) before going onto a rail or ledge.

C-Cut (hockey): Technique for backwards skating.

CE EN 1078: Approved standard for skate helmets.

Chassis: The 'blade' of the skate which holds the wheels.

Coping (aggressive): Round metal edge to ramps and all kind of transition surfaces.

Crash Shorts (aggressive): Fully padded shorts provide protection round the hips and base of the spine.

Crossover: Crossing one skate over the other to keep the power on when turning.

Death box (aggressive): A box designed to generate high airs on a street course.

Disaster (aggressive): Launching off a ramp before you pull a move – e.g. Disaster Royale.

Drills (hockey): Hockey practice exercises.

Driveway (aggressive): A box with flat banks both sides.

Double grab (aggressive): Two different grabs in the air before touching down.

Durometer: Hardness rating for a wheel.

Edges: Sides of the wheels in contact with the ground.

Fahrvervnügen (aggressive): Literally 'the joy of riding', and that is the correct way to spell a German word which comes out in all sorts of ways! In aggressive skating it's a grind with both knees bent in the same direction.

Fakie (aggressive): Riding backwards.

Fishbrain (aggressive): A topside Makio where the outside edge of the chassis is placed on top of the sliding surface, sliding forwards at high speed.

540 (rec & aggressive): One and a half rotations.

Flat bank (aggressive): A simple flat ramp or surface.

Flips (aggressive): An aerial move where the skater's body flips end over end.

Forehand (hockey): Handling the puck or ball with the front of the blade.

Frontside (aggressive): Grinding facing inwards such as on a kerb with your front to the pavement and back to the road, or on coping with the ramp behind you. A basic grind with the legs spread wide, grinding on the inside edges between the two middle wheels.

Fun box (aggressive): A multi-obstacle box on a street course.

Goal tender (hockey): The goalie or net minder.

Grab (aggressive): Grabbing a boot during a trick.

Grape Vine: A move combining 180 spins with skating backwards.

Grinding (aggressive): Sliding on the boot or chassis. Can be done on hand rails, coping, planters, benches, tops of walls and kerbs.

Grind Plate (aggressive): Reinforcing plate which bolts to the inside of the chassis for grinding between the middle two wheels. Plastic grind plates are favoured for a controlled, slower ride. Aluminium grind plates have less friction and give a much faster ride, and are only suitable for experts. Can be replaced on all skates.

Grind Wax (aggressive): Wax applied to curbs and other surfaces to make the skate slide more easily on its chassis.

Half pipe (aggressive): A large double ramp which looks like half a pipe when viewed side-on.

H-Block (aggressive): Removable H-shaped block which fits inside the chassis and gives extra support between the middle two wheels when grinding and stops the frame from wearing down.

Ho-Ho (aggressive): A two-handed invert – a handstand facing into the ramp.

IISS (aggressive): The International Inline Skate Series holds the world's major series of international aggressive events. It is related to the National Inline Skate Series (NISS) Tour in the USA.

Invert (aggressive): An invert hand-plant where the skater's legs go above the coping feet first.

ISHA (hockey): International Skater Hockey Association.

Juniors (hockey): 14-18 year old hockey players.

Line (aggressive): The route taken by a skater around a street course or vert ramp to link their tricks. Judges give marks for creative lines and using the course or ramp to its maximum potential.

Lui Kang (aggressive): A flying kick style of air move with one leg tucked up and the other extended. The tucked-up leg is grabbed as the other leg kicks out straight with no grab (the opposite of a Flying Fish). Named after a Mortal Kombat computer game character.

Marathons: Races usually held over 26.2 miles or 50 kilometres.

Method (aggressive): An air move with both legs pulled back behind the skater's body and one grabbed by the skater's hand.

McTwist (aggressive): A 540 spin in the air that goes inverted.

Mini ramp (aggressive): A small half pipe.

Minnows (hockey): Under 10 year old hockey players.

Mizou (aggressive): A grind with the leading skate grinding on the soul and the trailing skate grinding between the wheels.

Mute (aggressive): An air in which the skater grabs his chassis, bringing his knees tight to his chest.

Natural (aggressive): The natural way to turn – like being right-handed.

Negative rocker (aggressive): As for anti-rocker.

Negative soul (aggressive): The inside underside of the chassis which is used for 'soul grinding'. The outside underside is the soul area.

Net minder (hockey): The goalie or goal tender.

900 (rec & aggressive): Two and a half rotations.

Pace line (racing): A slipstream line of skaters in a race.

Pee-Wees (hockey): 10-14 year old hockey players.

Pick-up (hockey): The most relaxed form of hockey, usually played in the open with the absolute minimum of rules and restrictions.

Pivots (hockey): A technique which allows the player to change from forwards to backwards skating without losing speed.

Planter (aggressive): A decorative floral holder on the street used by skaters to grind on, or a purpose-built box rail in a skate park.

Pornstar (aggressive): A grind with the leading skate grinding on the soul and the trailing skate tucked in tight behind, boned over on the outside.

Positive rocker: Middle two wheels dropped down in chassis to provide faster turning when all four wheels are the same diameter. Mainly used on hockey skates.

Power skating: The skating stride.

Power slide: A high speed stop.

Power strap: An adjustable strap which either goes round the cuff of the boot or behind the heel and over the laces.

Puck (hockey): An ice hockey style disc which is used in place of a ball.

Pyramid (aggressive): A pyramid shaped box of ramps.

Quads: Conventional roller skates.

Quarter pipe (aggressive): A small curved ramp.

Rat Races: Races open to all abilities.

Ready position (hockey): The basic stance which allows a player to move in any direction in hockey.

Rink (hockey): The BSHA specifies a maximum size for a rink or pitch of 61 metres by 30 metres, with rounded corners and boards at least 80cm high. The minimum size for international matches is 40x20 metres.

Rocker: The ability to move wheels up or down in the chassis, either lowering the two middle wheels (hockey) or lifting them (aggressive).

Rocker spacers: Plastic or aluminium fittings which allow the wheel axles to be moved up or down in the chassis.

Rocket (aggressive): An air in which both legs are stretched out in front of the skater, facing the deck, grabbed by the toes.

Royale (aggressive): Grinding with the skates boned backwards as the skater slides forwards – i.e. chassis first followed by boot. The opposite of a fahrvervnügen.

Russian circles (hockey): A crossover practice routine for hockey.

Safety grab (aggressive): An air in which the skater grabs the top skate with his top hand as he turns, pulling both skates up to the side.

Seniors (hockey): Over 18 year old hockey players.

720 (rec & aggressive): Two complete rotations.

Shell: The plastic outer boot.

Shin Guards (aggressive & hockey): Extra protection for the vulnerable area between knee pads and skates.

Skate Jeans (aggressive): Cut wide and baggy from the knee to accommodate knee pads and shin pads with a flare to drop over top of skates and plenty of reinforcement. Can incorporate removable padding to protect hips and base of the spine.

Skate Paints: Scratch and chip-free paint applicators used to decorate faded skates and wheels.

Slap Shot (hockey): A shot at goal using a full swing.

Snap shot (hockey): Halfway between a slap shot and a wrist shot.

Soul (aggressive): The outside underside of the chassis which is used for 'soul grinding'. The inside underside is negative soul.

Soul Plate (aggressive): Reinforcing plate for soul (sole) area on outside of each boot. Used for grinding along the length of the skate on kerbs or rails. Can be replaced on some skates.

Spacer: Plastic or metal washer which divides the bearings in each wheel.

Spine (aggressive): The join when ramps are set back-to-back.

Spins (aggressive): Rotating in the air on skates. A spin can be from 360 to 1,080 degrees.

Sports Court (hockey): A purpose-built type of flooring using interlocking plastic tiles which is generally considered the best surface to play on.

Sprints: Short races, usually held over 300, 500 or 1,500 metres.

Stale Japan (aggressive): An under the body aerial grab – e.g. the left hand grabs the right leg.

Stick handling (hockey): Dribbling the puck or ball.

Stick tape (hockey): Used to cushion the handle of a hockey stick.

Street (aggressive): Aggressive tricks using ramps and other small-scale obstacles. Also a specific competition in aggressive events.

Stroking: Pushing with each leg to drive forwards.

Styling (aggressive): Making a trick look extra stylish.

Surfing: A move with the skates in line, heel to heel and toes pointing out.

Switch (aggressive): Unnatural – the opposite to natural which makes tricks more difficult.

Switch-ups (aggressive): Moving from trick to trick while grinding.

Teams (hockey): A team will usually consist of four players plus a goal tender on the pitch at any one time, drawn from a team of up to 16 outplayers and 2 goal tenders plus manager and coach.

1080 (rec & aggressive): Three rotations.

360 (rec & aggressive): A complete rotation, clockwise or anti-clockwise.

Time periods (hockey): A hockey game is divided into time periods, such as 2x15 minutes.

Topside (aggressive): 90 degrees to the sliding surface on a coping, rail or ledge.

Transition (aggressive): Changing moves.

T-Stop: Stopping by forming a T-shape with the skates.

Vert (aggressive): Aggressive skating using ramps with vertical surfaces – usually the half pipe.

Wrist guards: Safety gloves which support the wrists and protect the palms.

Wrist Shot (hockey): A shot at goal, using a quick wrist flick.

BISA (British Inline Skating Association)
PO Box 145, Bicester, Oxfordshire OX6 4HH
Tel/Fax: 01859 345 953.
Web Pages: http://www.demon.co.uk
nbesbisa.html
E-mail: skippy@dircon.co.uk

BFRS (British Federation of Roller Speed)
Events information c/o: Roller Speed, 4 Windsor Road, Castle Bromwich, Birmingham B36 0JN
Tel: 0121 770 7589 Fax: 0121 681 2737.

BSHA (British Skater Hockey Association)
Information, membership & enquiries: BSHA, PO Box 50, Hailsham, East Sussex B27 2BQ
Tel/Fax: 01323 440442.

BRHA (British Rink Hockey Association)
Scottish Region – Tel: 01389 757222.
North-West Region – Tel: 0161 799 2774.
North-East Region – Tel: 01724 783279.
Southern Region – Tel: 01705 793193.

BIPHA (British Inline Puck Hockey Association)
Information, membership & enquiries:
Tel: 01703 860 030

International Inline Skating Association (IISA)
3720 Farragut Avenue, Suite 400, Kensington, Maryland 20895 USA
Tel: 301 942 9770.

National Inline Hockey Association (NIHA)
999 Bricknell Avenue, 9th Floor, Miami, Florida 33131 USA
Tel: 305 358 8988
E mail: NIHAMIAMI@aol.com

National Inline Hockey Association (NIHA)
11810 Kingsway, Edmonton AB T5G OX5

Aggressive Skaters Association (ASA)
171 Pier Avenue, Suite 247
Santa Monica, California 90405 USA
Tel: 310 399 3436

USA Hockey Inline
4965 North 30th Street, Colorado Springs, Colorado 80919
Tel: 719 599 5500.

Acknowledgements

Jeremy Evans would like to thank the following for their help with this book.

In general:

Inline Skatermag for providing much of the background; **Adrian Parsons** of *Pacer Leisure* (**Inliners**) for his help, advice and loan of equipment; **Steve Glidewell** of *Unity* for his friendly advice on aggressive matters; **Ivan Solombrino** who skated so magnificently for the photos of all the recreational sequences; **Matt King** who skated equally magnificently for the photos of all the aggressive grinds and airs, and provided numerous other tricks for the book; and not least **Matt Pingel** for his excellent and very hard working photography which helps define this book.

In particular:

Brian Wood of *Roller Speed* for providing much of the information in *Speed Essentials* on pages 34-35; the **Oxford Wheels Project** for their help with *Get A Skate Park* on pages 42-43; **Matt King** for modelling and identifying the moves in *Kinds of Grinds* on pages 48-53 and *Airs & Grinds* on pages 54-61; **Andy Critchlowe** for his advice on aggressive disciplines and judging on pages 62-66; **David de la Haye** for providing information on *Pick-Up Hockey* on pages 70-71 and on hockey wheels on pages 76-77; **Bill Roche**, Coach to the *Swindon Eagles*, a mine of knowledge who provided most of the material for the other hockey pages and was a tremendous help; and **Mitch Heavey** of *Route One* in Kingston who provided much information for *Skate Maintenance* on pages 92-93.